KV-046-480

Seamanship International Ltd.

CARGO NTES

Dhananjay Swadi
Lecturer, Glasgow College of Nautical Studies

WITHDRAWN

LIVERPOOL JMU LIBRARY

3 1111 01218 5094

Dhananjay Swadi

Dhananjay Swadi has over 12 years experience at sea on a wide variety of ships, including container ships, gas tankers and bulk carriers, culminating as a Chief Officer with Maersk. In addition to his Masters licence, Mr. Swadi also has a Masters degree in Marine Policy with a distinction from Cardiff University of Wales. Until recently, Mr Swadi was a lecturer at the Glasgow College of Nautical Studies teaching a wide variety of subjects including Cargowork, Marine Law and Maritime Economics. In January 2006 he joined Northern Marine Management as Recruitment & Development Manager

First published 2005 by Seamanship International Ltd,
Willow House, Strathclyde Business Park
Lanarkshire, ML4 3PB. UK
Telephone: +44 (0) 1698 464333
E-mail: info@seamanship.com

Reprint 2006

© Seamanship International Ltd, 2005

All rights reserved. No part of this publication may be reproduced, stored in a retrieval system, or transmitted in any form or by any means, electronic, mechanical, photocopying, recording or otherwise, without the prior permission of the publishers,

While the advice given in this book (Cargo Notes) has been developed using the best information currently available, it is intended purely as guidance to be used at the user's own risk. Seamanship International accepts no responsibility for the accuracy of any information or advice given in the document or any omission from the document or for any consequence whatsoever resulting directly or indirectly from compliance with or adoption of guidance contained in the document even if caused by failure to exercise reasonable care.

This publication has been prepared to deal with the subject of Cargoes. This should not however, be taken to mean that this publication deals comprehensively with all of the issues that will need to be addressed or even, where a particular issue is addressed, that this publication sets out the only definitive view for all situations.

The opinions expressed are those of the author only and are not necessarily to be taken as the policies or views of any organisation with which he has any connection.

ISBN 1-905331-14-2

Issue 2

FOREWORD

'Cargo Notes', by Dhananjay Swadi, gathers together in one place a wealth of factual information that is taken from a variety of well respected and recognised sources, including official publications, concerned with the carriage and handling of cargoes. The information is presented in a logical and clear format comprising two well-indexed sections, the first on dry cargoes and the second on Liquid and Gas. Within each section the basic concepts behind safe carriage are first considered, and then progressively developed, to show the modern methods utilised in today's Shipping Industry.

Cargo Notes is ideally suited to seafarers preparing to sit written or oral examinations leading to Deck Officer Certificates of Competency. It is also a relevant reference work for on board usage and as a guide for cargo watch keeping Officers. It is an ideal companion to sister publications from Seamanship International on Seamanship and Ship Stability and is a worthwhile addition to any nautical library.

Richard Speight MSc FNI
Depute and Assistant Principal
Glasgow College of Nautical Studies
September 2005

CONTENTS

SECTION ONE: DRY CARGOES

SECTION TWO: LIQUID AND GAS CARGOES

ANNEXES

Principles and Operational Guidance for Deck Officers in Charge of a Watch in Port

INDEX

BIBLIOGRAPHY

SECTION ONE: DRY CARGOES

CARGO PLANNING

KEY POINTS

- A cargo plan provides information about the cargo and its location onboard the vessel

- An updated cargo plan must be available for reference in case of an emergency

- Cargo plans differ from trade to trade and, in certain cases, may need to be submitted in advance by the vessel to the port or terminal

- The Shipper must provide sufficient cargo related information in advance of loading for the vessel to prepare a viable cargo plan.

Information that is contained on a typical cargo plan:

- Name of the vessel

- Voyage number

- Loading port(s)

- Discharging port(s)

- Draughts for'd and aft

- Name of the Master

- Schematic of the vessel showing:
  - Location of cargo for different ports
  - Cargo quantities
  - Location of any dangerous or special cargo

Information that is required from the shipper[1]:

1. *In the case of general cargo and cargo carried in cargo units, a general description of the cargo, the gross mass of the cargo or cargo units and any relevant special properties of the cargo;*

2. *In the case of bulk cargoes, information on the stowage factor of the cargo, the trimming procedures, the likelihood of shifting, including angle of repose if applicable, and any other relevant special properties. In the case of a concentrate or other cargo which may liquefy, additional information in the form of a certificate indicating the moisture content of the cargo and its transportable moisture limit*

3. *In the case of bulk cargoes, information on any chemical properties that may create a potential hazard.*

---

[1] *Excerpted from SI 336; The Merchant Shipping (Carriage of Cargoes) Regulations 1999*

Using the information provided by the Shipper, the Master should ensure that:

1. The different commodities to be carried are compatible with each other or suitably separated

2. The cargo is suitable for the ship

3. The ship is suitable for the cargo

4. The cargo can be safely stowed and secured on board the ship and transported under all expected conditions during the intended voyage.

CARGO DOCUMENTATION

KEY POINTS

- Cargo documentation comes in various forms; some are mandatory and some because of commercial necessity.

- The documentation of a cargo consignment always follows the cargo.

- Each interchange of responsibility for the cargo is covered by a document

- Some cargo documentation is mandatory and required by legislation such as the IMDG code

---

When the cargo consignment is delivered to the terminal a *dock receipt* is issued to the person delivering it. This contains all relevant information about the cargo such as the weight, volume, number of pieces etc.

If any damage to the cargo is noticed at this delivery stage the dock receipt is so endorsed. This document is used to calculate the freight and other handling costs for the cargo.

When the cargo is transferred to the carrying vessel the terminal issues a *Mates Receipt,* which is then signed by the vessel. It is important at this stage to carefully note any damage to the cargo and endorse the Mates Receipt accordingly. A Mates Receipt should only be signed once it has been verified that the goods are actually loaded on board. On general cargo vessels this is usually done by comparing with the *tally sheets* made up by a *tally clerk*. In the container trade it is usually done by the shore agency of the carrier, who signs the Mates Receipts on behalf of the vessel's command.

The Mates Receipt is used to compile the *Bill of Lading (B/L)*. A B/L is the primary document that governs commercial transactions at sea. It performs three main functions, namely:

- It is a *receipt* for the goods carried

- It is *evidence* of the contract of carriage

- It is a *Document of Title*. This means that the holder of a Bill of Lading, in good faith, is entitled to the delivery of the cargo.

The B/L is generally endorsed according to the Mates Receipts. In many cases shippers require a clean B/L because of the requirements of their letters of credit, and may offer a *letter of indemnity* against a clean (unendorsed) B/L. The letter of indemnity has been proven to be of little value against a cargo claim. The best way to ensure a clean B/L is to ship undamaged cargo.

Bills of Lading can be of a number of different types. The main types in common use are as follows:

- **Negotiable Bill of Lading:** A document of title that can be transferred between persons or companies by endorsing in the proper place. The person that presents a suitably endorsed B/L at the discharge port gains possession of the cargo.

- **Straight Bill of Lading:** this type of a B/L cannot be transferred and only the named person, or his representative, can gain possession of the cargo at the discharge port.

- **Combined Transport Bill of Lading:** In the container trade, where one carrier often takes responsibility for the door-to-door transport of the cargo, this is a common type of B/L

- **Through Bill of Lading:** This is issued by the sea-carrier but states that he is responsible for the goods only during the sea passage part of the total transit.

- **Seaway bill:** this takes the same form as a B/L but is a non-negotiable receipt and not a document of title. This is usual in the container trade and is only a receipt for the goods carried and evidence of a contract between the shipper and the carrier. It does not need to be presented for delivery of the cargo.

A B/L has to be stamped and signed by the Master. In the container trade, due to the difficulty of presenting the B/L to the Master in time for the vessel to sail, the Master issues a letter, or power of attorney, to the carrier's agents authorising the agent to sign the Bills of Lading on his behalf.

The document used for customs clearance in the destination country is the *Cargo Manifest*. This is a comprehensive list of all cargo for that destination and is made up from information contained within the B/Ls.

A *Dangerous Goods Declaration* must be provided to the Master by the shipper of any goods that come under the auspices of the IMDG code[1].

A *Dangerous Goods Manifest* is compiled from bookings and provided to the vessel before loading commences. If necessary it is revised before sailing. This document lists the weight, quantity, packaging, class and stowage of all hazardous cargo on the vessel. It is compiled by the agent and signed by the master and agent.

---

[1] *See the section on the IMDG code for further information on this*

Example of a Bill of Lading

OCEAN BILL OF LADING

SIAM INTERNATIONAL FREIGHTLINES

SHIPPER/EXPORTER	BOOKING NO.
MR. VORAVIT KOSOL 1100 S.W. CLAY STREET PORTLAND, OR 97201 U.S.A.	LAXBGK D 03628 **EXPORT REFERENCES** 04380/BKK

CONSIGNEE	FORWARDING AGENT FMC NO
MR. VORAVIT KOSOL 18/1 COVENT ROAD SILOM, BANGKOK THAILAND	SIAM INTERNATIONAL FREIGHLINE OTI NO. 12475NF **POINT AND COUNTRY OF ORIGIN OF GOODS** PORTLAND

NOTIFY PARTY	ALSO NOTIFY – ROUTING AND INSTRUCTIONS
SAME AS ABOVE' 635 3443	TRIUMPH INTERFREIGHT 537/197 SATHUPRADIT COMPLEX YANNAWA BANGKOK THAILAND TEL: 2942095

• INITIAL CARRIAGE BY	• PLACE OF INITIAL RECEIPT PORTLAND	
EXPORTING CARRIER APL ENGLAND V 103	PORT OF LOADING LONG BEACH	LOADING PIER TERMINAL
AIR/SEA PORT OF DISCHARGE BANGKOK THAILAND	• PLACE OF DELIVERY BY ON CARRIER	TYPE OF MOVE

PARTICULARS FURNISHED BY SHIPPER

MARKS AND NUMBERS	NO. OF PKGS.	HM	DESCRIPTION OF PACKAGES AND GOODS	GROSS WEIGHT	MEASUREMENTS
VORAVIT KOSOL BANGKOK THAILAND	61 BOXES (3SKIDS)		SAID TO CONTAIN: 61 CARTONS OF USED HOUSEHOLD AND PERSONAL EFFECTS FREIGHT PREPAID SKID DIMENSION: 53 x 40 x 69 INCHES (LxWxH) 48 x 42 x 52 INCHES 50 x 48 x 59 INCHES	2680LBS CLEAN ONBOARD V/V APL ENGLAND V103 DATED: JUL15,2001	227.25CUF & .435CBM

SHIPPERS DECLARED VALUE $ _____ SUBJECT TO EXTRA FREIGHT
AS PER TARIFF AND CARRIERS LIMITS REFER TO CLAUSE 16 HEREOF
FREIGHT PAYABLE AT BY

FREIGHT CHARGES	PREPAID	COLLECT
227.25 CUF X 4.00 PER CUF	$ 909.00	
TOTAL CHARGES		

Received the goods, or packages said to contain goods herein mentioned, in apparent good order and condition unless otherwise indicated, to be transported and delivered, to trans-shipped as herein provided. The carriage is subject to the provisions of the U.S. Carriage of Goods by Sea Act of 1936. All the terms and conditions of the Carrier's regular form Bill of Lading, as filed with the Federal Maritime Commission available to any shipper or consignee upon request, are incorporated with the force and effect as if they were written at length herein, and all such terms and conditions so incorporated by reference are agreed by Shipper to be binding and to govern the relations, whatever they may be between those included in the words "Shipper" and "Carrier" as defined in Carriers regular form Bill of Lading.

IN WITNESS WHEREOF, the Carrier has signed and the Shipper has received THREE (3) original bills of lading, ONE of which being accomplished, the others to stand void.

Dated At _____ SIAM INTERNATIONAL FREIGHTLINES   AS CARRIER

By NANCY S.

MO JUL DAY 15 YEAR 2001

BL. No. 04380/BKK

• APPLICABLE ONLY WHEN DOCUMENT USED AS A THROUGH BILL OF LADING

13

14

CARGO WATCHKEEPING

KEY POINTS

- Keeping an efficient and safe cargo watch is a key requirement of an OOW.

- STCW'95, Chapter 8, states that cargo watchkeeping is a key requirement for watchkeeping in port.

Cargo Responsibilities

The Cargo Officers are responsible for the safe and efficient handling and stowage of cargo, for the correct preparation of cargo spaces and for the correct supervision of its loading. The officers should liase with other ship staff and key members of shore staff i.e. foremen, tally clerks, terminal operators etc.

Checks to be made prior to the cargo being loaded

1. Check that holds are clean, dry and ready to receive the cargo. If any dunnage is laid, it should be inspected

2. Hold inspection should include the inspection of plating, access ladders, lighting, guard rails, storm valves and pipes, fire fighting gear and fittings, manhole covers, spar ceiling, etc.

3. Check that all lifting plant (derricks, cranes, wires, blocks etc) are in good order and properly rigged. Check all cargo gear is certificated and tested. Ensure that a proper risk assessment is in place prior to using the lifting gear.

4. All lashing gear must be in place and inspected, as is described in the *Cargo Securing Manual* section of this book.

Checks to be made during loading to ensure that the cargo is not damaged:

1. Check acceptability of the cargo. The cargo must be dry and in apparent good condition. Check for damages. If the cargo is sensitive to moisture ensure proper conditions throughout loading are maintained. Close hatches during rain where necessary.

2. Visually check the cargo while it is being loaded. Inspect the cargo for damage. Cargo may have been subject to damage while in transit to the dock, on the quayside or during loading. Damage to cargo may be caused by incorrect stowage or slinging, careless use of mechanical handling equipment e.g. forklift trucks, insufficient attention to labelling and marking, carelessly packed units, insufficient dunnaging or packaging, incorrect ventilation settings, or wrong set points in case of refrigerated cargo.

3. Check correct handling and use of cargo handling equipment. For example, cargo hooks should never be used when discharging fragile cargo.

4. The Cargo Officer must be familiar with the ships' specialised cargo gear.

5. Check cargo sling arrangements to safeguard against the cargo being dropped or wrong Safe Working Load (SWL) slings being used.

6. The stowage of all cargo should be checked with reference to the cargo plan. Particular attention should be paid to the loading of dangerous or refrigerated cargo. Reefers must be plugged in immediately and the temperature noted.

7. When stowing general cargo preventative measures should be taken to ensure against the possibility of fragile goods being crushed when stowed with heavy goods.

8. Some cargoes are liable to damage from taint. These should not be stowed next to strong smelling cargoes.

Procedure for dealing with damaged cargo:

If any discrepancies with the condition of the cargo appear a Cargo Damage or Exception Form should be filled out and given to the stevedores prior to the ship sailing. The Master should report any discrepancies associated with the quantity of cargo loaded or discharged on a letter of protest.

The Cargo Damage Report is a statement of damage to the cargo that gives all of the details. Damage reports should have certain essential items recorded on them e.g. cargo marks, commodity type, container type and number involved, stowage location, when discovered, extent of damage and the time of the discovery. It may be necessary to get the damage surveyed prior to loading or even to reject the cargo in serious cases.

Checks after completion of cargo

1. All cargo securing arrangements and lashings should be checked as necessary. Check all lashing gear is in good order. Check bottom tiers of containers are secure and that twist locks are in position and locked before subsequent tiers are loaded.

2. When cargo operations are finished for the day hatches should be closed and secured for sea.

3. The amount of cargo worked that day should be recorded and the draughts fore, aft and amidships taken and recorded in the Deck Logbook.

4. Throughout the cargo watch a notebook should be carried and a note of all salient occurrences made e.g. times when heavy lifts loaded, times when work commences and ceases at each of the hatches, number of

gangs onboard, times when deck lashings checked, completion times for hatches, etc. These notes will then be transferred to the Deck Logbook and will be compared with the shore tally sheet.

Besides the items above, the watchkeeping officer is responsible for a whole range of activities including monitoring safety, pollution prevention and other matters related with watchkeeping in port.

Relevant extracts from STCW'95 Chapter 8 *Watchkeeping in Port* are included in the appendix and should be referred to in addition to the above.

HOLD PREPARATION

KEY POINTS

- Before loading, the cargo spaces should be inspected and prepared for the particular material that they are intended to load.

- Preparation should also include inspection of ancillary equipment like bilges, sounding pipes and other service lines within the cargo space.

A charter party or contract of carriage normally requires the owner to *"... make the holds, refrigerating and cooling chambers and all other parts of the ship where goods are carried, fit and safe for their reception, carriage and preservation."* The owner is also required to present the holds "clean and dry" prior to commencement of loading. If the owner fails to present his ship in a fit state to receive the cargo, he risks cargo contamination claims amounting to large sums of money. It is, therefore, of the utmost importance that the owner makes all efforts to prepare the cargo holds of his ship prior to loading.

The preparation of the holds that is carried out for the next cargo depends on a number of factors:

- What the last cargo carried was

- What the requirements of the next cargo are

- The time available

- The equipment and manpower available

If the next cargo is compatible with the last, a good sweep down and removal of leftover cargo is all that is required. If, however, the next cargo is incompatible with the last or if you are loading sensitive cargoes like foodstuffs, a more thorough cleaning may be required.

The following is a hold cleaning sequence that is generally followed on bulk carriers:

1. Remove all residues of the previous cargo. Sweeping down and collecting cargo residues for removal usually achieves this.

2. Any dunnage that is left over in the holds is stacked and removed.

3. Holds are then usually washed with seawater and, if required, with a final rinse of fresh water. A fresh water rinse can reduce corrosion and accelerate drying. Special attention needs to be given to remove residues from areas that can be difficult to reach, such as hatch covers and frames.

4. Bilges and strum boxes are to be properly cleaned and, if necessary, the bilge area is to be disinfected or lime washed. Bilges are then covered with burlap to prevent entry of cargo particles.

5. Hold inspection to be carried out and any damages repaired

6. Ancillary systems, like the fixed fire fighting equipment or ventilation equipment, must be tested.

7. New dunnage should be laid out if required.

8. Hold lighting to be checked

9. Means of access should be checked for damage and must be free of any hazards.

10. Cargo gear must be checked and rigged for loading or discharge.

11. Hatch covers must be examined for weather tight integrity and, if necessary, the rubber packing renewed.

12. Fumigation is to be carried out if the Charterers or cargo owners require it. The IMO publication *"Recommendations on the safe use of pesticides at sea"* and MGN 284 *"Recommendation for ships carrying fumigated bulk cargoes"* must be referred to.

13. Air pipes, fixtures and fittings must be checked and any repairs carried out.

USE OF DUNNAGE

KEY POINTS

- Dunnage is the name given to material that is used to protect goods and their packaging from moisture, contamination or mechanical damage.

- Dunnage can be wood, plastic, tarpaulin or a range of other materials

- On some types of ships permanent dunnage may be fitted.

The word "dunnage" is an old sailing term for material placed between cargoes to prevent shifting.

Uses of dunnage:

- To provide protection to the cargo from water damage caused by contact with water from the bilges, other cargo or double bottom tanks.

- It protects moisture-sensitive cargoes, such as bagged cargo (e.g. coffee, cocoa) or bales (e.g. tobacco, tea) from sweat, which forms on a ship's sides and runs off over the decks.

- To provide air channels between stows to aid ventilation, mainly for refrigerated cargoes.

- To prevent damage to goods through contact with either the ship's structure or with other cargo.

- To aid in the effective distribution of weight on tank tops or hatch covers.

- To aid in filling void spaces between cargoes, especially unevenly shaped cargoes.

Dunnage maybe divided into floor, lateral, interlayer and top dunnage.

Floor dunnage is mainly used in general cargo ships to lift the cargo off the tank top. This prevents cargo damage from sweat or moisture running off from other cargo. Floor dunnage is laid crosswise and the direction depends on the design of the vessel. In ships with lateral water drainage (bilges), the first layer must be laid crosswise, while in ships with fore and aft water drainage (wells), the first layer must be laid lengthwise. Such dunnage should be laid close together to prevent the cargo from making contact with the tank top. On modern vessels, especially reefers, permanent deck gratings are fitted made of grooved and perforated aluminium or plywood gratings are fitted.

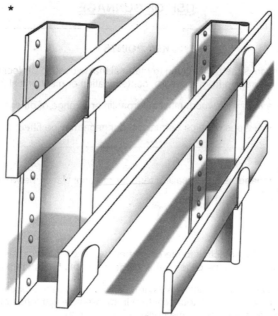

Lateral dunnage usually takes the shape of a *spar ceiling* on a general cargo vessel. These are wooden beams that are securely connected to the side of the cargo hold. Later dunnage prevents contact of the cargo with the ship side and thus prevents cargo damage due to sweat. In the absence of spar ceilings, wooden dunnage or criss-cross dunnage must be used. This criss-cross dunnage consists of nailed grids, cross-wise wooden dunnage being nailed to vertical uprights (vertically positioned squared beams).

Permanent Collapsible Dunnage (PCD's) comprising painted or varnished 8' x 4' plywood sheets may be fitted to the ship's sides. These sheets are hinged at their base and open out to be secured in a variety of ways. Their main purpose is to "square off" curved ship sides and they are particularly useful for palletised cargo.

Interlayer dunnage separates cargoes from each other. This is either for the protection of an underlying cargo from contamination by a top cargo or for the segregation of individual batches of cargo.

Top dunnage generally protects the cargo from contamination damage from water, hydraulic oil, etc., dripping from the weather decks. Top dunnage must also allow for some air circulation and evaporation, especially for hygroscopic cargoes. For this reason top dunnage is usually made from an air permeable material such as paper or jute

---

* Reprinted from Cargo Work by DJ House, published by Elsevier

Any wooden dunnage used must be dry to prevent moisture damage. The "*Transport Information Service (TIS)*" from the German Insurance Association (GDV e.V.) recommends a water content of no more than 12 -15%, air dried[1]. Any wooden dunnage that is too fresh or has been exposed to the atmosphere must not be used.

On modern reefer vessels increasing use is being made of inflatable dunnage. This has the advantage of being re-usable and it is inflated as required using compressed air, which is readily available on board.

Dunnage is also used within freight containers to prevent sweat damage. As standard containers cannot be easily ventilated, humidity levels inside can rise and significant amounts of moisture can condense on the sides and the bottom. To prevent damage to the cargo top, side and bottom dunnage is used. This can be moisture absorbent paper, timber to chock and secure the cargo on the sides, or plastic tarpaulins. The tarpaulins are suspended under the container ceiling (not in contact with the cargo if at all possible) and have "reservoirs" in which the sweat may collect as it drips (*GDV -Transport Information Service*).

---

[1] http://www.tis-gdv.de/ - cargo information – dunnage.

SEPARATION AND MARKING OF CARGO

KEY POINTS

- It is often necessary to separate different parcels of the same cargo
- Methods of separation differ from trade to trade
- Break-bulk cargo is often stencilled with individual identifying marks

---

Types of Separation

On general cargo ships, parcels of the same cargo for discharge to different ports are often separated. Some of the more common means of separation include:

- Coloured Polythene sheets

- Burlap: This is often used as a separation for bagged cargoes in the break-bulk trade.

- Tarpaulin: This can be used to separate cargoes such as bulk grain particularly on handy sized bulk carriers.

- Cargo nets: Polypropylene mesh nets can be used to separate cargo parcels in the same hold.

- Paint: Timber can be separated by paint, usually water based. Steel rails and coils can be separated by paint or coloured tape

- Marking tape: On a ro-ro vessels, cars of the same type for discharge at different ports are often separated using either "hazard" tape or coloured marking tape.

Marking of cargo

To prevent over carriage[1] and to allow freight forwarders to correctly identify cargoes, most break bulk cargoes are labelled or stencilled with identifying marks. These marks can form a part of the Bill of Lading[2] description of the cargo.

---

[1] *Inadvertent carriage of cargoes to the next port.*
[2] *See the section "Cargo Documentation" for the types of Bills ofLading (B/L)*

CARGO VENTILATION

KEY POINTS

- Moisture damage can be a source of significant cargo claims.

- Most of these claims are as a result of a failure to correctly ventilate the cargo hold causing cargo sweat or ship sweat.

Ships may be fitted with natural or forced ventilation systems. These may be used for the following:

- To prevent cargo or ship sweat

- For the removal of taint or smell of previous cargoes

- To prevent the build-up of dangerous gasses

- To supply fresh air to "live" cargoes

- For the removal of the heat that is given off by certain cargoes

When using the ventilation system to prevent ship or cargo sweat, continuous monitoring of the hold atmosphere must be carried out. This is because the moisture content of the cargo, coupled with variations in air temperature, cargo temperature and sea temperature, can dramatically influence the amounts of water vapour retained by and released into the air inside a hold[1].

Types of cargoes affected:

Hygroscopic cargoes: Hygroscopic products have natural moisture content and are mainly of plant origin. They may retain, absorb or release water vapour, and excessive amounts of inherent moisture may lead to significant self-heating and "moisture migration" within the cargo. This can result in caking, mildew or rot. Examples of hygroscopic products include grain, rice, flour, sugar, cotton, tobacco, cocoa, coffee and tea.

Non-hygroscopic products: Non-hygroscopic products have no water content. However, certain commodities (eg steel) may be damaged if stowed in a moist environment. Others may be harmed if packaged using a hygroscopic material (eg wood, paper)

Types of Sweat

Cargo sweat: Cargo sweat refers to the condensation that may form on exposed surfaces of the cargo as a consequence of large amounts of warm, moist air being introduced into a hold containing substantially colder cargo. This usually occurs when the voyage is from a colder to a warmer place and the outside air

---

[1] www.westpandi.com; loss prevention bulletin; February 2000

has a *dewpoint*[2] above the temperature of the cargo. To prevent this sweat forming all ventilation should be restricted until the temperature of the cargo is above the dewpoint temperature of the outside air.

Ship's sweat: Ship's sweat refers to condensation that forms directly on a vessel's structure when the air within a hold, made warm and moist by the cargo, comes into contact with cold surfaces as the vessel moves into cooler climates. Cargo may be damaged by overhead drips, by contact with sweat that has formed on the ship's sides or by condensed water that may accumulate at the bottom of the hold. To prevent ship sweat, holds should be surface ventilated as long as the dewpoint of the outside air is lower than the temperature of the air inside.

If the dewpoint of both the outside and the hold air can be determined then the West of England P&I club[3] advises the use of the *"Dewpoint Rule"*:

- *VENTILATE if the dewpoint of the air inside the hold is higher than the dewpoint of the air outside the hold.*

- *DO NOT VENTILATE if the dewpoint of the air inside the hold is lower than the dewpoint of the air outside the hold.*

The *three degrees rule* may be applied when it is impracticable to measure hold dewpoint temperatures accurately. In such cases ventilation requirements may be estimated by, several times a day, comparing the average cargo temperature at the time of loading with the outside air temperature. Ventilation may then be carried out on the following basis:

- *VENTILATE if the dry bulb temperature of the outside air is at least 3°C cooler than the average cargo temperature at the time of loading.*

- *DO NOT VENTILATE if the dry bulb temperature of the outside air is less than 3°C cooler than the average cargo temperature at the time of loading or warmer.*

In order to apply the Three Degree Rule, it will be necessary for the ship's staff to take a number of cargo temperature readings during loading.

In addition to ventilating the holds, regular hold inspections should be carried out whenever possible.

In general terms, hygroscopic cargoes require to be monitored more carefully than non-hygroscopic cargoes. Ventilation is rarely required if only non-hygroscopic cargoes are carried. As far as possible, hygroscopic and non-hygroscopic cargoes should not be stowed together due to the differing ventilation requirements.

Proper records and logs must be maintained in order to defend against cargo claims.

---

[2] *When an isolated volume of air cools, relative humidity increases as the temperature falls. Once the temperature has descended to the level at which saturation occurs water begins to condense. This temperature is known as the "dewpoint". This is generally measured by wet and dry bulb thermometers or by "whirling psychrometer".*
[3] *www.westpandi.com; loss prevention bulletin; February 2000*

$$S.f = \frac{1}{D} \qquad D = \frac{m}{v}$$

STOWAGE FACTOR AND BROKEN STOWAGE

KEY POINTS

- Stowage factor is the ratio of weight to stowage space required under normal conditions

- Broken stowage is the space lost due to the uneven shape of the cargo or unavoidable gaps in cargo stowage, expressed as a percentage of the total volume of the cargo.

Stowage Factor

This is the space occupied by a unit weight of cargo under normal conditions. A ship has a limited amount of space in which to load the cargo. The stowage factor of the cargo will allow calculation of the space this cargo will occupy in the hold, given the weight of the cargo. The lower the stowage factor the denser the cargo. For example, iron ore has a stowage factor of 0.28 m^3/t whereas cotton waste has a stowage factor of 2.78 m^3/t. The stowage factor of the same type of cargo may vary depending on the nature of cargo and the region from where it is sourced. Where bale goods are concerned an important point is whether the bales are carried compressed or uncompressed. For example, hemp in bales uncompressed has a stowage factor of 7.3 m^3/t whereas the same cargo compressed has a stowage factor of 2.55 – 3.4 m^3/t.

Relationship Between Weight, Volume and Stowage Factor

Stowage Factor is the volume occupied by a unit weight of cargo. Therefore, to convert a given weight to the corresponding volume, we use the following:

Volume (m^3) = Weight (tons) X Stowage Factor (SF) (m^3/t)

Broken Stowage

This is the space lost due either to the uneven nature of the cargo or to the packaging or dunnage between cargoes.

It is often expressed as a percentage of the volume of the cargo and will vary with the nature of the cargo carried.

Calculation Examples

1. A 250 tonnes parcel of palletised cargo has an SF of 1.8m³/t. Allowing for 5% broken stowage, calculate the space this parcel of cargo will occupy in a hold.

    Note;   V= Wt x SF; Wt = V/SF; SF = V/Wt

    Volume Occupied 250x1.8 = 450 m³
    5% Broken stowage = 5%x450 = 22.5 m³
    *Space occupied = 450 + 22.5 = **472.5 m³***

    (Alternatively 105% x 450 = 472.5m³)

2. If the parcel is placed in a hold of 1200m³ bale capacity, calculate the space remaining for other cargo.

    Space available =   1200.0 m³

    *Space remaining= 1200-472.5   =**727.5 m³***

3. Calculate the weight of cargo, SF 1.3m³/t BS 5% that may be loaded in the remaining space.

    The space remaining = 105% of the volume of cargo to load

    727.5m³ = 105% x Volume of cargo

    $\frac{727.5}{105\%}$ = Volume of cargo to load

    Volume of cargo to load = 692.86m³

    *Wt of cargo to load = $\frac{692.86m³}{1.3m³ /t}$ = **532.97t***

CARGO GEAR: DERRICKS

KEY POINTS

- General Cargo vessels tend to have their own gear to load and discharge cargoes

- Cargo derricks come in a variety of designs and safe working loads

---

Many General Cargo vessels have their own cargo gear that helps them to load and discharge in ports lacking infrastructure. This cargo gear is usually in the form of a derrick or crane serving each hold and is often a distinguishing feature of General Cargo ships.

Single Swinging Derrick

The basic form of cargo gear is the single derrick. This can be equipped with span tackles & cargo purchases.

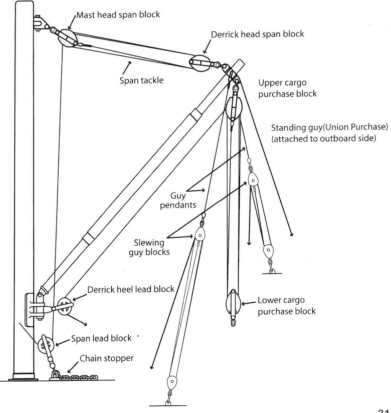

The span blocks are secured to the mast of the derrick head and the "topping wire" is permanently fitted on to a winch. The operation of this winch raises or lowers the derrick boom. The "runner wire" runs through the upper and lower cargo blocks and the "slewing wire" runs through slewing guy blocks on either side of the derrick. In its most basic form the derrick is plumbed over the hatch square and secured. The cargo is then lifted with the runner blocks and the slewing guys are operated to swing the derrick and discharge the cargo over the side. As the cargo purchase, the topping lift and the two guys must operate independently, 4 independent winches are needed to operate this type of derrick.

Union Purchase Derrick

One of the most efficient rigs is the Union Purchase Derrick. Union Purchase means a rig in which a pair of derricks is used in combination, the derricks being fixed and the cargo runners coupled.

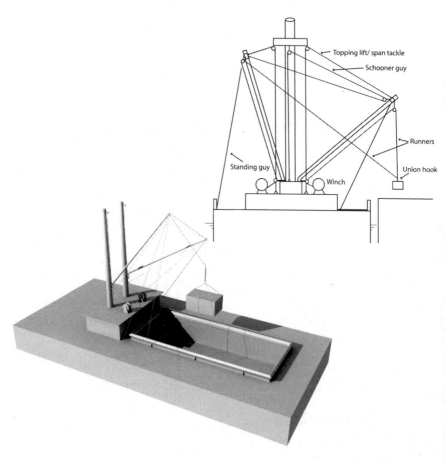

One derrick plumbs the hatch and the other plumbs overside. The falls of the two derricks are fastened together at the cargo hook. One derrick boom is arranged over the hold and the other is overside. The booms are then fixed in position. When the vessel is discharging cargo, the derrick that is plumbing the hold lifts the load. After the load has been lifted over the hatch coamings it is gradually transferred to the fall from the other derrick, which is plumbing overside. This is done by heaving on one fall and slacking on the other. To avoid overstressing the rig the angle between the falls should not exceed 90 degrees and never exceed 120 degrees. Due to the coordination required in slacking one fall and heaving the other, only experienced operators must be employed. Union Purchase can become an extremely fast method of loading/discharging cargo in units of up to about 1½ tonnes each, but it has the disadvantage of placing heavy stresses on the outboard guys of both derricks, hence additional static *preventer (standing) guys*. There is not a great deal of stress on the inboard guys but these must be set taut to prevent the derrick jerking. As an alternative to inboard guys a *schooner guy* may be rigged between the derrick boom heads (as shown above), thus reducing deck clutter.

Precautions:

When using the derricks in the union purchase mode the maximum load must not exceed either one-third the SWL of the lowest rated derrick in the pair or an absolute maximum of 2.5 tonnes. Narrow angles between the outboard guys and the vertical should be avoided as this increases the load on them. However, the angle should not be too large as this increases the chance of the derrick jack-knifing. Also, as stated above, the angle between the falls should not exceed 90 degrees and should never exceed 120 degrees to avoid undue stresses on the rig.

Doubling Gear

As previously stated, when using derricks in a Union Purchase Rig the maximum load must not exceed one thirds the SWL of the lowest rated derrick. Therefore, if there is a requirement to lift a load heavier than the SWL of the union rig but less than that of the SWL of an individual derrick, the rig can be unhitched and the single derrick can be used as a swinging derrick. If the item's weight is close to or in excess of the SWL of the cargo runner, it may be lifted by "*doubling up*" the cargo runner so that the stress limit is not exceeded.

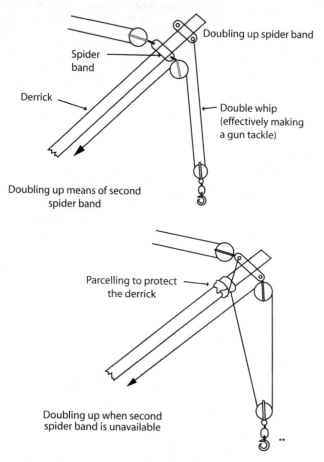

Doubling up spider band

Spider band

Derrick

Double whip (effectively making a gun tackle)

Doubling up means of second spider band

Parcelling to protect the derrick

Doubling up when second spider band is unavailable

Doubling up the runner in this way will allow the lifting of a weight in excess of the SWL of the runner if rigged as a *single whip*. It does NOT however permit the lifting of a weight in excess of the SWL of the lifting appliance as a whole.

** Reprinted from Seamanship Techniques by DJ House, published by Elsevier.

Velle Derrick

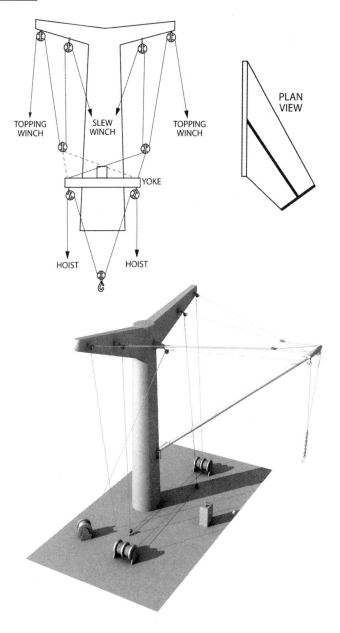

PLAN VIEW

TOPPING WINCH

SLEW WINCH

TOPPING WINCH

YOKE

HOIST

HOIST

The Velle derrick is a patent derrick that has been popular on general cargo vessels built in the 1970's. This is a single swinging derrick, the distinguishing feature of which is 'T' bar or 'floating bridle bar' at the derrick head, to which the cargo hoist head blocks and topping spans blocks are secured. The advantage of this arrangement is that it allows a greater slewing radius and the "T" bar provides stability when discharging or loading containers or heavy lifts.

Two winches, each with separate barrels, control topping and slewing. Two lengths of wire are used leading from the topping winch barrels to the slewing winch barrels. On the topping winch the barrels turn in the same direction and, on operation of either, the boom tops or lowers. On the slewing winch barrels they are wound in opposite directions and on operation the derrick slews, while maintaining the derrick head at a constant level. A third winch with twin barrels, both wound in the same direction, is used as the hoisting winch.

Advantages:

- It is relatively easy to operate by comparison to a swinging derrick

- It is a one man operation

- The 'T ' bar helps to stabilise loads and prevents them from swinging

- There is less clutter in comparison with a traditional derrick

- The SWL is from 25 to 100 tonnes

Hallen Derrick

The Hallen is another patent design in common use. This derrick has a "D" frame mast with outrigger rods. The 'D' Frame has the effect of maintaining a satisfactory angle between the twin topping lifts, allowing control and stability of the derrick when swung out over the ships side, even to an angle of about 80^0 to the fore and aft line. The outrigger rods prevent contact between the topping lift pennants and the "D" frame when the derrick is slewed to its maximum outboard angle.

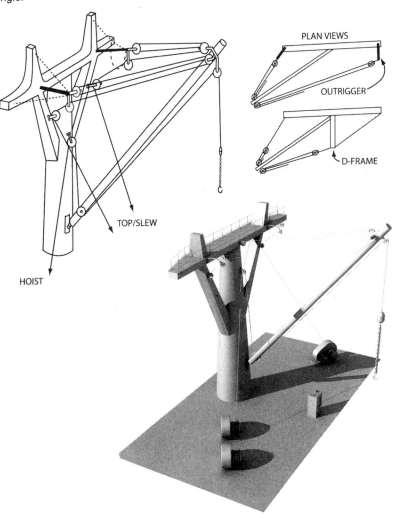

PLAN VIEWS

OUTRIGGER

D-FRAME

TOP/SLEW

HOIST

Each topping lift has its own winch but both are usually controlled by one multi-position control. Topping is achieved by operating both winches in the same direction. Slewing is achieved by heaving on the winch at the side to which the derrick is to go and slacking on the other. A third winch controls the cargo purchase. Alternatively, an arrangement similar to that employed by the Velle derrick can be used.

Advantages

- It is simple in comparison with a single swinging derrick.

- It uses a One-man operation of lifting, slewing and hoisting.

- It operates with up to 15^0 of List.

- It can operate down to 15^0 above the horizontal.

- Slewing angles are as much as 80 degrees.

- The deck area is clear of clutter.

- It has up to 200 Tonne capacity, with only the cargo hoist to be changed to operate quickly for lighter loads.

Stulken Heavy Lift Derrick

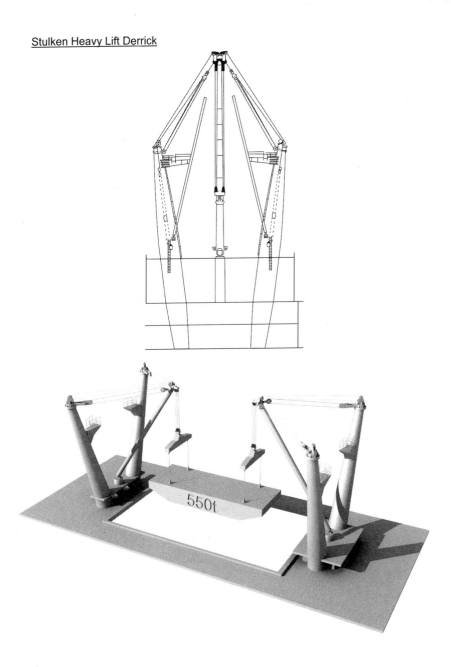

The Stulken derrick was patented in 1954 by Blohm & Voss in Germany and has since that time has been fitted to hundreds of ships. The V shaped inclined masts support the derrick and allow a wide arc of operation.

The derrick can be swung between the masts so as to service either of the two adjacent hatches.

Four winches operate the lifting plant, two for the hoist and one for each span. The hoisting winch has two gears to enable a faster operation when lifting relatively lighter loads.

One person can operate the derrick either by using a remote control or by standing on a specially constructed platform.

Advantages:

- It is permanently rigged and so there is not much preparation time before use
- It has sealed bearings, which are low maintenance and reduce friction.
- Additional derricks suitable for a union purchase arrangement can be fixed on to the same inclined masts.
- It is constructed of low weight high strength steel
- It is a one man operation, using a remote if necessary
- Safe working loads of up to 800 tonnes are possible

CARGO GEAR: CRANES

KEY POINTS

- Cranes have largely replaced derricks as cargo gear onboard modern ships

- Modern cranes are low maintenance, versatile and, in the case of gantry cranes, mobile along the length of the ships

---

Pedestal Cranes

Shipboard Pedestal Cranes rotate on a pedestal and are permanently mounted on a ship. The main housing consists of the operator's cabin, winches, and the jib, which projects from the pedestal. The crane is either electrically or hydraulically operated and the housing rotates on the pedestal. There are usually two winches inside the housing, one for the topping of the jib and the other for the hoist. Both are controlled, from inside the cabin using a joystick.

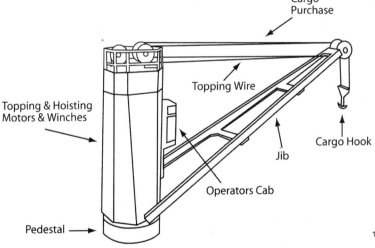

Advantages

- 360 degree rotation
- Good spot loading
- Fast operation
- Low maintenance
- The SWL of two cranes may be combined when used together.
- Grabs, container spreaders etc. can be fitted to the cargo hook.

---

[1] *www.mcgregor-group.com*

Safety Features

- Limit switches for topping and hoisting

- Jib angle indicator, indicates the angle of the jib which corresponds to the SWL

- Two block limit switch, prevents the inadvert contact of the floating runner block and the jib mounted runner block

- Slack wire cut off

- SWL cut off prevents a weight in excess of the SWL from being lifted

- Topping and hoisting winch cut off, that cuts off the power when less than 3 turns remain on the winches or if the wires become fouled.

- A flashing light placed at the end of the jib to prevent accidental contact with shore cranes.

Shipboard Gantry Cranes

The basic design of gantry cranes consist of steel girders across the beam of a vessel supported by legs and travelling on rails mounted on the ship's decks. The gantry houses the operators' cabin as well as the lifting mechanism and it can travel athwartships on the bridge girders. The whole gantry can travel fore and aft on wheels mounted at the base of the gantry. Hydraulic buffers at the ends of the rails prevent the crane from over-running the rails.

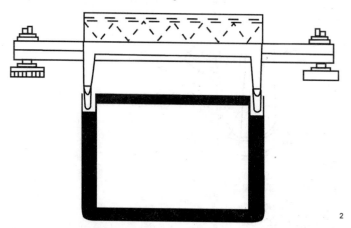

2

Shelters that allow the cargo operation to be carried out, even during light rain, can cover this type of crane. These are usually fitted onto ships loading and discharging weather critical cargo, such as plywood or paper products. Prior to

---

[2] www.gearbulk.com

bringing the crane into operation, hinged outriggers are swung out, allowing the discharge or loading of products over the ships' side. Usually these outriggers are hydraulically operated and have a mechanism to lock them in place. Prior to sailing the outriggers are folded in and locked onto the side of the girders.

The other type of gantry crane in use is the *jib type* crane. The main difference is the jib that is mounted on the bridge girders. In some types the jib can travel athwartships along the bridge girders while in other models the jib is fixed in the centre. In both cases the jib swings from port to starboard and the operator's cabin is mounted on the jib. This type of gantry crane is used on small feeder container ships as the container spreader at the end of the jib can be used to load and discharge cargo from a very stable base.

Advantages of gantry cranes

- Mobile over the length of the deck
- Unobstructed view for the operator
- Shelters may be fitted to protect cargo during handling operations
- Reduced possibility of load rotation due to box shaped girders
- Fast operation possible with experienced operators

Safety Features

- Klaxon and light when moving along the deck
- Maximum safe trim cut-out
- Emergency stop switch at deck level
- Hydraulic buffer at the end of deck rails
- Two block limit switch
- Slack wire limit switch
- Maximum SWL limit switch
- Outrigger cut-outs if not locked in place
- "Cow-catcher" safety guards on the wheels, which cut out the power if they hit an obstruction.

LIFTING PLANT: TESTING & CERTIFICATION

KEY POINTS

- Lifting plant must be checked prior to use and tested at regular intervals

- Trained and certificated personnel must operate lifting plant

- Cranes and derricks must be maintained as per manufacturers' instructions.

Training & Certification

All cargo gear must only be operated by personnel who have received appropriate training in the operation of the plant. As a means of verification a certificate may be issued. A risk assessment must be carried out prior to using the cargo gear for the first time and, based on the findings, appropriate control measures must be put in place.

Testing, Maintenance & Examination of Lifting Plant

Ships cranes and derricks should be properly operated and maintained in accordance with manufacturers' instructions. Sufficient technical information must be available on board, including the following:

- Rigging Plans
- SWL of all fittings
- Boom limiting angles
- Manufacturers' instructions for replacing wires & sheaves

Prior to use, a visual inspection must be carried out keeping the following points in view:

- Checks for any leaks of hydraulic oil
- Worn or damaged wires
- Excessive corrosion
- Cracking at welds
- Missing marking

All control units, joysticks, alarms and limit switches must be checked prior to use and all controls must be operated before attaching the slings or grabs to the crane or derrick. Any slings to be used must be inspected and must be of sufficient SWL.

Banksman

Trained personnel should direct the lifting plant operator using agreed and generally understood means of communication. The Code of Safe working Practices for Merchant Seamen contains a list of approved hand signals that must be used.

Testing & Certification

The *'Merchant Shipping (Hatches and Lifting Plant) Regulations 1988'* require the following for testing and certification of the Lifting Plant:

- A Test using an approved proof load, which may be greater than the Safe Working Load (SWL) of the lifting plant, must be carried out

    o After installation of the plant

    o After repair or alteration likely to affect SWL

    o At least every 5 years.

- A Thorough Examination, which must include some dismantling for inspection, must be carried out by a Competent Person (someone with sufficient theoretical and practical knowledge)

    o At least every 12 months

    o After a statutory test.

Certificates & Reports

The Master must ensure that a certificate or report is on board within 28 days of any statutory test or examination and that the certificate remains on board for at least two years following the receipt of the next certificate. Certificates and reports should be kept readily available on board and copies of the latest certificates should be made available to any shore worker using the ship's lifting plant.

Certificates and reports should be in the form approved by the Secretary of State and based on the internationally agreed form prepared by the International Labour Organisation (ILO).

A *Register of Lifting Appliances and Cargo Handling Gear* should be maintained in a form recommended by the ILO. The register may be in paper or electronic form.

Annex 7.1

CERTIFICATE OF TEST AND THOROUGH EXAMINATION OF LIFTING APPLIANCES

Name of Ship   Certificate No. ....

Official Number

Call sign

Port of Registry

Name of Owner

(1) Situation and description of lifting application (with distinguishing numbers or marks, if any) which have been tested and thoroughly examined	(2) Angle to the horizontal or radius at which test load applied	(3) Test load (tonnes)	(4) Safe working load (SWL) at angle or radius shown in column (2) (tonnes)

Name and address of the firm or competent
person who witnessed testing and carried out   ....
thorough examination   ....
                                                      ....

I certify that on the date to which I have appended my signature, the gear shown in column (1) was tested and thoroughly examined and no defects or permanent deformation were found; and that the safe working load is as shown.

Date: ....   Signature: ....
Place: ....

Note: This certificate is the standard international form as recommended by the International Labour Office in accordance with ILO Convention No. 152.

Marking of Lifting Equipment

Each lifting appliance and item of lifting gear must be clearly marked with:

- Its Safe Working Load (SWL)
- A means of identification

If it is not practical for the SWL to be marked on the item, it must be made readily ascertainable by some other means. Where the SWL of a crane varies with operating radius, an indicator clearly showing the SWL at any given radius must be fitted.

The SWL of an appliance that is normally used with a specific attachment (e.g., a spreader or clamp) should specify whether the weight of the attachment is included in the SWL. Any item of lifting gear weighing a significant proportion of the overall SWL must be clearly marked with its weight in addition to its SWL. Slings supplied in batches must bear the same identification mark.

In the case of multi-legged sling assemblies, the marking should specify the SWL up to an angle of 90^0 between:

- Opposite legs, in the case of two-legged slings
- Adjacent legs, in the case of three-legged slings
- Diagonally opposite legs, in the case of four-legged slings

There may be a further SWL up to a maximum angle of 120^0.

HEAVY LIFT PRECAUTIONS

KEY POINTS

- A risk assessment must be done prior to a heavy lift.
- The critical stage is when the weight has been lifted off the ground by the ship's lifting gear.
- It is important to have adequate stability prior to the operation and to avoid any slack tanks.

A heavy lift operation must always be well planned and carried out with the utmost care. A risk assessment must be carried out and a permit to work system must be in operation. In any heavy lift operation the critical stage, when using ships' lifting gear, is when the load has just cleared the ground. The weight of the load then acts as if it has been placed on top of the lifting gear and this causes a rise in the ship's centre of gravity. Initial stability must be adequate to avoid a situation where the ship's centre of gravity rises above its transverse metacentre, causing a capsizing lever to form. The ship will also heel when the load is lifted up and any slack tanks will create a free surface effect, causing a further rise in the centre of gravity. The entire operation must be carried out slowly and using experienced operators. The lifting hook must be exactly above the load to avoid the load dragging on the ground and swinging, causing excessive strain on the lifting gear. The Port Authority must be informed prior to the operation so that any passing traffic can be asked to slow down. The following is a list of things to check before and during this critical operation:

- Ensure the vessel is as near as possible to upright and calculate the maximum heel during operation.
- Avoid any slack tanks.
- Lay out dunnage to spread the load and protect the ship/cargo.
- Check deck or tank top load-limit.
- Lifting gear certificates must be in order & the SWL sufficient.
- Lifting points must be satisfactory.
- Any slings used must have an adequate SWL
- Steadying lines are to be attached to prevent the load swinging.
- The accommodation ladder / gangway is to be attended.
- Sufficient crew, wearing PPE, to attend to mooring lines
- Fenders rigged and barges etc. cast off
- Railings removed if required.

- Adequate power on deck.
- Communications established.
- Non-essential personnel are cleared from the working area.
- Operators are fully certificated
- Lifting hook is plumb above the load.
- Weight must be taken slowly.
- Relevant signals should be displayed and the Port Authority informed.

THE CARGO STOWAGE & SECURING CODE (CSS)

KEY POINTS

- The purpose of the code is to provide an international standard to promote the safe stowage and securing of cargoes.

- This is as per the 1996 amendments to chapter VI and VII of SOLAS

- The CSS code gives stowage and securing guidance on a variety of cargoes both on deck and under deck.

The general principles of stowage and securing of cargoes, as described in the CSS code are as follows:

Cargo Stowage and Securing

- Cargoes are to be stowed and secured so that the ship and persons on board are not at risk

- Stowage and securing should be planned, executed and monitored properly

- Personnel carrying out the tasks should be qualified and experienced

- Personnel planning and executing the tasks should have a sound practical knowledge of the application and content of the *Cargo Securing Manual*[1].

- Improper stowage and securing will be hazardous to other cargoes and the ship

- Stowage and securing must be planned with the most severe weather conditions that could be expected on the voyage in mind

- Ship handling decisions in bad weather must be carefully considered.

The CSS code lists the following criteria for estimating the risk of a cargo shift:

- The dimensional and physical properties of the cargo

- Location of the cargo and the stowage on board

- Suitability of the ship for the cargo

- Suitability of the securing arrangements

- Expected seasonal weather conditions

---

[1] *See the chapter on Cargo Securing Manual*

- Expected ship behaviour during the voyage
- Stability of the ship
- Geographical area of the voyage
- Duration of the voyage

These criteria, along with the fact that some cargoes have a tendency to compact themselves during the voyage or have a low coefficient of friction, must be taken into account when selecting suitable stowage and securing methods. The Master should only accept cargoes if he is satisfied that they can be safely carried.

After evaluating the risk of the cargo shifting, the Master should ensure prior to loading that:

- The deck area is clean and free of grease and oil

- The cargo is in a suitable condition for transport

- All necessary cargo securing equipment is on board

- Cargo that is either in or on cargo transport units or vehicles is properly secured to those vehicles or units

The CSS Code in line with SOLAS Chapter VI and VII requires the carriage on board of an approved *Cargo Securing Manual*. The cargo securing arrangements in this manual should be based on the forces expected to affect the cargo carried by the ship, calculated either in accordance with the method described in Annex 13 of the CSS code or an acceptable alternative.

Chapter 2 of the CSS Code details the principles of safe stowage and securing of cargoes. This deals with the following points:

- Suitability of cargo for transport
- Cargo distribution
- Cargo securing arrangements
- Residual strength after wear and tear
- Friction forces
- Shipboard supervision and inspection

Chapters 3 and 4 deal with standardised and semi standardised stowage and securing. This includes securing arrangements and the stowage and securing of vehicles.

Chapter 5 deals with non-standardised stowage and securing. This includes advice for cargoes not covered by chapters 3 and 4, particularly those cargoes that are difficult to stow or that have proved to be a potential source of danger. These include cargoes such as:

- Containers on non-cellular ships
- Portable tanks & receptacles
- Special wheel based cargoes
- Heavy cargoes
- Coiled sheet steel
- Heavy metal products
- Anchor chains
- Scrap metal in bulk
- Flexible intermediate bulk containers
- Logs in under deck stow

Chapter 6 deals with actions to be taken in heavy weather and gives advice on the measures to avoid excessive acceleration:

- Alteration of course or speed
- Heaving to
- Early avoidance of areas of adverse weather
- Timely ballasting and deballasting to improve the ship's behaviour
- Voyage planning to avoid areas of severe weather and sea conditions.

Chapter 7 deals with actions that may be taken once a cargo has shifted. The code recommends the following actions for consideration:

- Alterations of course
- Reductions of speed
- Monitoring the integrity of the ship
- Restowing or resecuring the cargo
- Increasing friction
- Diversion of route or seeking shelter

13 annexes then follow these chapters. The first 12 annexes deal with the safe stowage and securing of cargoes that are a potential source of danger, as detailed in Chapter 5 of the Code. Annex 13 deals with methods to assess the efficiency of securing arrangements for non-standardised cargoes, including the provision of guidance for the preparation of the Cargo Securing Manual.

Annex 13 also gives a *Rule-of-thumb* method for securing cargoes:

> "The total of the Maximum Securing Load (MSL)[2] values of the securing devices on each side of a unit of cargo (port as well as starboard) should equal the weight of the unit"

This method does not take into account the adverse effects of lashing angles, non-homogenous distribution of forces among the securing devices or the favourable effect of friction. The code recommends that the transverse lashing angles to the deck should not be greater than 60° and that adequate friction is provided by the use of suitable materials.

The code recommends a *safety factor* to be used in calculations to take into account the possibility of uneven distribution of forces among the devices or reduced capability due to improper assembly of the devices. The safety factor gives the calculated strength (CS) from the MSL as follows:

$$CS \; = \; \frac{MSL}{Safety\ Factor}$$

---

[2] **Maximum securing load** is a term to define the load capacity used to secure cargo to a ship. Safe working load (SWL) may be substituted for the MSL provided this is equal to or exceeds the strength defined by MSL.

CARGO SECURING MANUAL

KEY POINTS

- SOLAS requires certain vessels to have a ship specific Cargo Securing Manual approved by the Flag State.

- *SI 336 Carriage of Cargoes Regulations* makes it mandatory on UK vessels other than bulk carriers.

SOLAS Chapter VI and VII requires a Cargo Securing Manual (CSM) to be aboard all types of ships, other than solid and liquid bulk, engaged in the carriage of cargoes.

Cargo units and cargo transport units must be loaded, stowed and secured throughout the voyage in accordance with this manual.

Cargo Securing Manual

For UK flag vessels *SI 336 Carriage of Cargoes Regulations* states that:

"All passenger ships and cargo ships carrying cargoes other than solid bulk cargoes, except cargo ships of less than 500 tons engaged on voyages which are not international voyages, shall carry on board a Cargo Securing Manual."

The approved Cargo Securing Manual must conform to the guidelines developed by the IMO. All securing devices must meet acceptable functional and strength criteria applicable to the ship and its cargo. All crew engaged in the stowage and securing of cargo must be trained and instructed in the safe and efficient operation of the lashing and securing devices.

Key Definitions:

Maximum Securing Load (MSL) *is* a term used to define the allowable load capacity for a device used to secure cargo to a ship.

Safe Working Load (SWL) may be substituted for MSL for securing purposes, provided this is equal to or exceeds the strength defined by MSL.

Standardized Cargo means cargo for which the ship is provided with an approved securing system, based upon cargo units of specific types.

Semi-standardized Cargo means cargo for which the ship is provided with a securing system capable of accommodating a limited variety of cargo units, such as vehicles, trailers, etc.

Non-standardized Cargo means cargo that requires individual stowage and securing arrangements.

Chapter 1 contains general statements dealing with the requirement to practice good seamanship and the requirement to maintain all securing devices to a good standard. It also specifies a minimum quantity of spares to be carried on board.

Chapter 2 gives details of the specifications of fixed and portable securing devices and their maintenance schemes. This should give as much detail as possible about the securing devices in use *on that ship*. Plans or sketches can be used to illustrate the type, location and total number of securing devices on board.

Chapter 3 provides handling and safety instructions and an evaluation of the forces acting on the cargo transport units using tables and diagrams of those forces acting on the cargo in relation to the metacentric height. This chapter also draws the Master's attention to the correct application of portable securing devices, taking into account factors such as:

- Duration of the voyage

- Geographical area of the voyage, with particular regard to the minimum safe operational temperature of the portable securing devices

- Sea conditions that may be expected

- Dimensions, design and characteristics of the ship

- Expected static and dynamic forces during the voyage

- Type and packaging of cargo units, including vehicles

- Intended stowage pattern of the cargo units including vehicles mass and the dimensions of the cargo units and vehicles.

Chapter 4 contains handling, safety, stowage and securing instructions for containers and other standardised cargoes. It illustrates allowable stowage patterns, evaluation of forces acting on cargo transport units and principles of stowage and securing both on deck and under deck. Stowage and securing plans must be available illustrating, among other things, stowage patterns, the maximum stack weight limitations and permitted stack heights.

It contains further information on the nominal increase of forces or accelerations with an increase of initial stability. Recommendations should be given for reducing the risk of cargo losses from deck stowage by restrictions to stack masses or stack heights where high initial stability cannot be avoided.

Inspection and maintenance schemes, as required by the IMO guidelines, can be contained in a separate document provided this is clearly referenced in the Cargo Securing Manual. Ship specific handling and safety instructions must be included and these should contain the results of a risk assessment, if one was carried out.

The shipper is also required to supply cargo specific information to the Master so that he can evaluate the suitability of the cargo for the ship and make decisions on the stowage and securing.

TIMBER DECK CARGOES

KEY POINTS

• Timber cargoes carried on deck can shift and cause damage to vessels and can result in the ship capsizing

• International rules are in place to safely stow and carry timber cargoes on deck

In response to a increasing number of incidents of casualties related to a shift of timber cargo carried on deck, the IMO published the *"Code of Safe Practice for Ships Carrying Timber Deck Cargoes."* This publication is required to be on board on all UK vessels as per *SI 336 Carriage of Cargoes Regulations (1999)*.

Code of Safe Practice for Ships Carrying Timber Deck Cargoes, 1991

The purpose of the code is to make recommendations on the stowage, securing and other safety matters related to the carriage of timber on deck. The code applies to ships of length greater than 24 metres

Key Definitions:

Timber means sawn wood or lumber, cants, logs, poles, pulpwood and all other type of timber in loose or packaged forms. The term does not include wood pulp or similar cargo.

Timber deck cargo means a cargo of timber carried on an uncovered part of a freeboard or superstructure deck.

Timber load line means a special load line assigned to ships complying with certain conditions related to their construction as set out in the *International Convention on Load Lines*. It is used when the cargo complies with the stowage and securing conditions of the *Code of Safe Practice for Ships Carrying Timber Deck Cargoes*.

Weather deck means the uppermost complete deck exposed to weather and sea.

Stability Requirements:

The ship should be supplied with comprehensive stability information that takes into account the timber deck cargo. Such information should enable the master to quickly obtain accurate guidance as to the stability of the ship under varying conditions of service. Comprehensive rolling period tables or diagrams have proved to be a very useful aid in verifying the actual stability conditions.

The stability at all times should be positive and the following should be among the factors to be taken into account:

The increased weight of the timber deck cargo due to:

- Absorption of water in dried or seasoned timber
- Ice accretion, if applicable
- Variations in consumables, such as oil or water
- The free surface effect of liquid in tanks
- Weight of water trapped in broken spaces within the timber deck cargo and especially logs.

Before proceeding to sea the Master should ensure that:

- The ship is upright
- The ship has an adequate metacentric height
- The ship meets the required stability criteria.

The loading should immediately cease if an unexplained list develops. The *Merchant Shipping (Load Line) Regulations 1998* allow an initial GM of 0.05 metres, provided the timber is stowed and secured as per the code. This is because the buoyancy of timber contributes to the reserve buoyancy of the ship and so the ship can sail with a lower initial GM. Excessive stability should also be avoided as this creates racking stresses and increases the stresses on the lashing and securing system. The code recommends that the metacentric height should, by preference, not exceed 3% of the beam, although this can vary from ship to ship.

Some ships are allocated with timber load lines. Such ships are only allowed to load to this load line provided the lashing and securing requirements of the code and the applicable regulations of the Load Line Convention are followed *(The Merchant Shipping (Load Line) Regulations 1998, Part IV)*.

Stowage Considerations

The *"Code of Safe Practice for Ships carrying Timber Deck* Cargoes" recommends the following to be checked prior to loading timber on the weather deck:

- Hatch covers, and other openings to spaces below that area, should be securely closed and battened down
- Air pipes and ventilators should be efficiently protected and check valves or similar devices should be examined to ascertain their effectiveness against the entry of water

- Accumulations of ice and snow on such areas should be removed

- It is preferable to have all deck lashings, uprights, etc., in position before loading. This will be necessary should a pre-loading examination of securing equipment be required in the loading port.

- Ensure that access to all areas of the ship regularly used in the necessary working of the ship is not impeded.

During loading, the timber deck cargo should be kept free of any accumulations of ice and snow. Upon completion of loading, but before sailing, a thorough inspection of the ship should be carried out. Soundings should also be taken to verify that no structural damage has occurred, causing ingress of water.

The height of timber cargo should be restricted to ensure that:

- Adequate visibility is assured

- A safe margin of stability is maintained at all stages of the voyage

- Cargo does not overhang the ship side

- The weight of the timber deck cargo does not exceed the designed maximum permissible load on the weather deck and hatches.

For ships provided with and making use of their timber load lines, the cargo should be stowed so as to extend:

- Over the entire available length of the well or wells between superstructures and as close as practicable to end bulkheads

- At least to the after end of the aftermost hatchway in the case where there is no limiting superstructure at the aft end

- Athwartships as close as possible to the ship sides, after making due allowance for obstructions such as guard rails, bulwark stays, uprights, pilot boarding access, etc. This is provided that any area of broken stowage thus created at the side of the ship does not exceed a mean of 4% of the breadth

- To at least the standard height of a superstructure other than a raised quarterdeck.

The basic principle is that there should be a solid stow during all stages of the loading process. This can only be achieved by the constant supervision of responsible officers.

<u>Securing:</u>

Every lashing should pass over the timber deck cargo and be shackled to independent eye plates that are adequate for the intended purpose and then efficiently attached to the deck stringer plate or other strengthened points. They should be installed in such a manner as to be, as far as is practicable, in contact with the timber deck cargo throughout its full height.

All lashings and components used for securing should:

- Possess a breaking strength of not less than 133 kN[1]

- After initial stressing, show an elongation of not more than 5% at 80% of their breaking strength

- Show no permanent deformation after having been subjected to a proof load of not less than 40% of their original breaking strength.

Every lashing should be provided with a tightening device or systems so placed that it can safely and efficiently operate when required. The load to be produced by the tightening device or system should not be less than:

- 27 kN in the horizontal part

- 16 kN in the vertical part.

After completion of lashing there should be at least half the threaded length of screw available for tightening during the voyage. The spacing of the lashings should be such that the two lashings at each end of each length of continuous deck stow are positioned as close as practicable to the extreme end of the timber deck cargo.

Timber uprights should be fitted when required by the nature height or type of timber carried. When fitted, uprights should be:

- Of adequate strength

- Fitted at intervals not exceeding 3 metres

- Secured adequately to the deck.

Lashings should be spaced depending on the height of the cargo.

- for a height of 4 m and below, the spacing should be 3 m

- for heights of above 4 m, the spacing should be 1.5 m.

Rounded angle pieces of suitable material and design should be used along the upper outboard edge of the stow to bear the stress of the lashings.

---

1. One Newton equals 0.225 lbs. force or 0.1 kgf.

If the timber deck cargo is stowed over the hatches and higher, it should, in addition to being secured by the lashings recommended, be in a system of athwart ship lashings (*hog lashings*) joining each port and starboard pair of uprights near the top of the stow and at other appropriate levels as appropriate for the height of the stow:

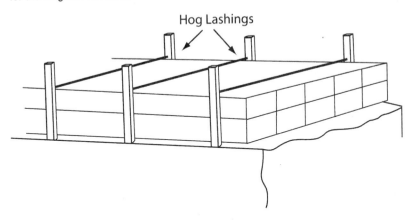

Hog Lashings

A lashing system to tighten the stow, whereby a dual continuous wire rope (*wiggle wire*) is passed from side to side over the cargo and held continuously through a series of snatch blocks, can also be used. The dual continuous wire rope should be led to a winch or other tensioning device to facilitate further tightening. This can also be used as a quick release mechanism in order to jettison the cargo in case of an emergency.

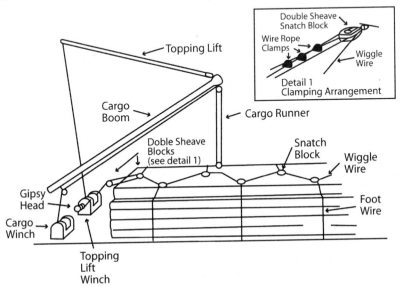

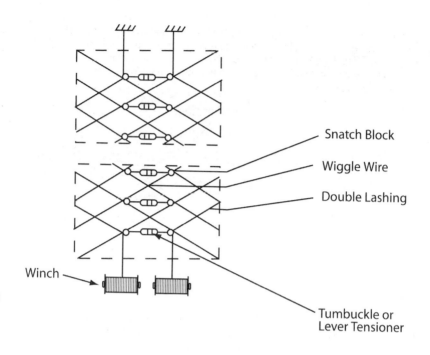

Snatch Block

Wiggle Wire

Double Lashing

Winch

Tumbuckle or
Lever Tensioner

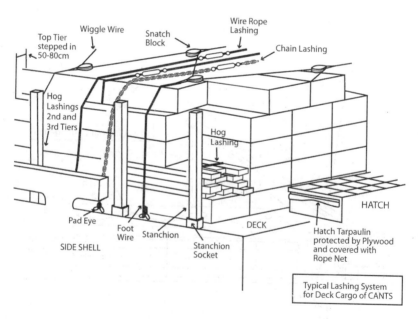

Top Tier
stepped in
50-80cm

Wiggle Wire

Snatch
Block

Wire Rope
Lashing

Chain Lashing

Hog
Lashings
2nd and
3rd Tiers

Hog
Lashing

Pad Eye

Foot
Wire

Stanchion

Stanchion
Socket

SIDE SHELL

DECK

HATCH

Hatch Tarpaulin
protected by Plywood
and covered with
Rope Net

Typical Lashing System
for Deck Cargo of CANTS

All lashings and securing devices used must be tested and certified. A record must be maintained of all certificates, testing and inspection dates. As per the recommendations of the code, lashing plans must be provided to the ship and these must be available for inspection.

On completion of lashing, a walkway or other means of access must be provided to required areas of the ship without endangering the lives of crewmembers.

Prior to sailing and immediately after sailing all lashings must be examined and tightened as the vibration of the ship may have caused them to loosen. Records of all checks and adjustments to lashings must be maintained in the ships logbook.

The Master must ensure that proper weather routeing is carried out so as to avoid areas of bad weather and high swell. In case of bad weather causing the jettisoning or loss of cargo appropriate reports must be made to the nearest coastal state, as per Chapter V of SOLAS.

CONTAINER CARGOES

KEY POINTS

- Containerisation and door to door transport has revolutionised world trade

- Correct securing and stowage of containers and cargoes within containers is vitally important

One of the most important ship types to come into existence after World War 2 was the container ship. The man credited with starting the container revolution is Malcolm Mclean, a road transport operator from the US. He converted two tankers to carry trailers and sailed from New York to Houston in 1956[1]. Since then containerisation has revolutionised world trade and commerce as the benefits of containerisation over general cargo ships are many. The cargo in the container can be transported from door to door and this has reduced warehousing costs and increased security in transit. Time in port was minimised and the port labour costs were also reduced due to the lower numbers of people required for loading and unloading a cellular container ship. The main disadvantages are the increased capital costs in building specialised ships and terminals and the increased investment in specialised IT systems to track and locate containers.

Ship sizes have increased substantially in the past few years and ships of more than 8000 TEU[2] are increasingly common. It has been predicted that by 2010, several ships with a capacity of 15,000 TEU's will be in operation. They will be up to 450 metres long, 70 metres wide and will carry 24 rows of containers. With the ship size increasing there has been a corresponding increase in incidents of cargo losses due to containers being swept overboard in bad weather. The wide variety of container types can also create a problem as the biggest container ship can carry more refrigerated cargoes than a conventional reefer ship and more chemical and dangerous cargoes than a small chemical tanker.

Container sizes have been standardised since the 1960's and, except for a few specialised types of containers, the majority of containers are of either 20 feet by 8 feet by $8^{1/2}$ feet or 40 feet by 8 feet by $8^{1/2}$ feet. The majority of container ships in existence are *cellular* ships. This means that the containers fit in slots under deck and do not need additional lashing or securing if carried under deck. A few conventional ships are also able to carry containers but they need to be secured under deck using chains or wires.

---

[1] http://www.oceansatlas.com/transportation/dry-cargo-ships
[2] TEU: Twenty foot equivalent unit, this is the amount of empty twenty foot boxes that the ship can carry and is a measurement of volume.

20 Foot Dry

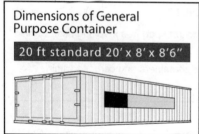

Weight: 2300 Kgs
Max Payload: 28180 Kg
Max Gross weight: 30480Kg
Cubic Capacity: 33.2m^3

40 Foot Dry

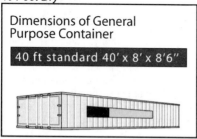

Weight: 3750Kgs
Max Payload: 28750 Kg
Max Gross weight: 32500 Kg
Cubic Capacity: 67.7 m^3

40 Foot High Cube

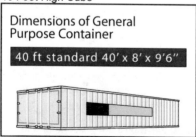

Dimensions similar to above except
the height is 9' 6"
Cubic Capacity: 76.4 m^3

20 Foot Reefer

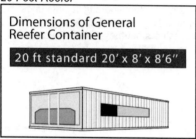

Dimensions similar to the 20 foot dry
container above, except the cubic
capacity reduces to 28.3 m^3 due to
insulation.

Container Stowage

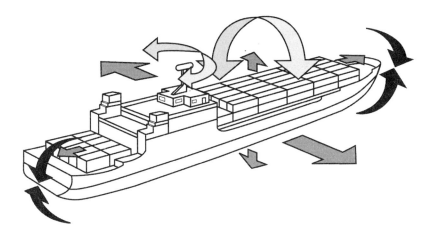

Containers are mainly stowed lengthwise as the loading capacity of the side walls is greater than the ends. Also, in a seaway, the stresses are usually greater athwartships than in a fore and aft direction. On some conventional ships containers may be stowed athwartships. Care must be taken to ensure access between containers for checking, lashing and unloading. Containers, when stowed on deck, are exposed to the stresses caused by the vessel moving in a seaway and are also exposed to wind stresses. The main principle in container stowage is ensuring a compact stow in all cases.

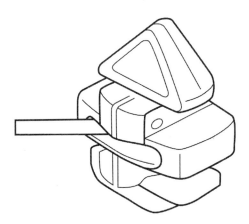

Manual Twistlock

In a semi-automatic twistlock a spring-loaded mechanism automatically locks the twistlock in place. Other containers in the same tier have intermediate twistlocks fitted that lock them onto the container immediately below. The containers are then held together over the entire width of the ship or the hatch-cover using cross lashings tightened by turnbuckles.

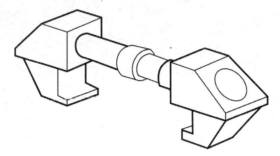

To complete the stow, *bridgefittings* may be fitted on the top row. These are attached to adjoining containers and serve the purpose of compacting the stow. However, in modern ships bridge fittings have become rare as the heights of stows have increased, making it dangerous to manually fit in bridge fittings on the top tier.

Any lashing system in place must be approved by the flag state or a designated classification society. All approved lashing systems will be found in the *Cargo Securing Manual* along with the maintenance procedures. On conventional vessels additional lashing equipment may be also used.

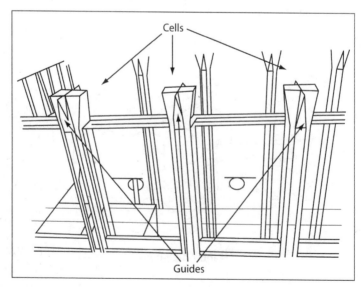

For under deck stowage on cellular ships *cell guides* are constructed from the tank top to the top of the hold. These guides are the width of a standard container and the boxes are slotted in place. Usually no other lashing is required, perhaps with the exception of *stacking cones* between container tiers.

For conventional ships that are adapted to carry containers, a number of different systems are in existence. Since the holds are not adapted to carry containers they have to be lashed using bridge fittings and cross lashed using chains. The following diagram from *The Container Handbook*[3] illustrates underdeck lashing of containers on a conventional ship using bridge fittings, stacking cones, twistlocks and chain lashings for the bottom two tiers.

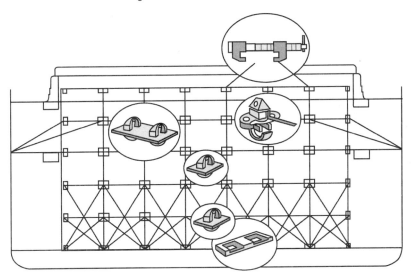

Container Stowage Planning

It is important to be able to locate the position of each individual container on board a ship in order to effectively plan the loading and discharging. To enable this containers are usually stowed following the *bay-row-tier* method. The ship is divided lengthwise into bays which are numbered from fore towards aft in the following manner:

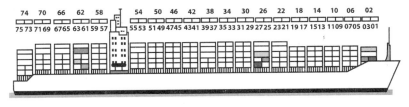

---

[3] *http://www.containerhandbuch.de/chb_e/stra/index.html?/chb_e/stra/stra_01_01_00.html*

Odd numbered bays are for 20 foot containers while even numbered bays are for 40 foot containers. One 40 foot bay can be divided into two 20 foot bays. For example, if the stowage plan refers to Bay 02 then the container in question is 40 foot in length whilst if the plan refers to Bay 01 or Bay 03, the container is 20 foot in length.

To plan athwartships stowage the containers are divided into *rows* and *tiers*. The rows of containers on a ship are numbered with even numbers from the centre towards the port side and odd numbers from the centre towards the starboard side. In case of an odd number of rows the centre row is numbered "00"

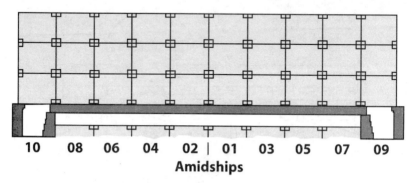

| 10 | 08 | 06 | 04 | 02 | 01 | 03 | 05 | 07 | 09 |

Amidships

Tiers are numbered in the following manner:

On deck, *the bottom tier is numbered "82", the one above is tier 84 and so on.*

Underdeck *the bottom tier is tier "02" the one above tier 04 and so on as illustrated in the following diagram.*

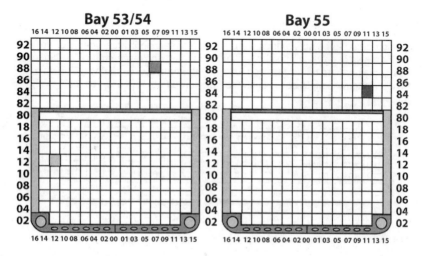

The containers are always referred to in the "bay-row-tier" format. For example, using the above diagram a 20 foot container stowed underdeck (shaded) will be referred to as Bay 53, Row 12, Tier 12; or 531212 in short. On deck the shaded container on Bay 54 (40 Feet) will be referred to as 540788; and the 20 foot box on Bay 55 will be 551184.

To illustrate the containers on a cargo plan *Bay-plans* are used. Each bay plan shows the cell and a tier number for each container space and provides space for container codes and weight information. The container codes help to identify the container in that space. The weight information helps the planner distribute the weight of the containers and enter this into the stability computer. Once familiar with the container codes used in the bay plan, cargo watch keepers will be able to read the bay plans to locate and identify the containers in them. Container codes consist of a port code, a container serial number and the container weight.

Duties of the OOW

Following are some of the issues and items that the OOW must consider when loading containers:

- Understand and review the stowage plan

- Be aware of special requirements for containers containing dangerous goods, including their stowage, segregation and marking

- Reefer containers are to be placed in their correct slots and their temperatures monitored as per the manifest

- Check that any over-height or over-width cargoes are properly stowed.

- Check lashings for breakbulk cargo stowed on containers

- Check that stack limits not exceeded

- Note any physical damage to the containers

- Check that the door seal is intact

- Check for leaks or other evidence of cargo damage

- Ensure that the lashing plan is correctly followed

- Attend to the ballast to ensure that the ship remains upright and with a reasonable trim by the stern

- Check all lashings on completion

- Keep proper records

RO-RO VESSELS STOWAGE AND SECURING

KEY POINTS

- In a Ro-Ro vessel correct stowage and securing of wheeled cargo is vital for safety reasons.

- HMSO publishes a code of practice that provides guidance and information on safe procedures to be followed on board these vessels.

Cargo stowage and securing is a vital aspect of Ro-Ro vessel operations. To reduce the risks inherent in the loading, securing and carriage of cargoes on such vessels, guidelines are given in the "*Roll-on/Roll-off ships –stowage and securing of vehicles – code of practice*" published by HMSO. The *Code of Safe Practice for Cargo Stowage and Securing (CSS Code)* published by the IMO, also gives guidance on securing and stowage of all cargo. It is mandatory that this is carried onboard UK flag vessels. The ship should also have on board an approved *Cargo Securing Manual,* in accordance with regulations VI/5 and VII/6 of SOLAS 1974.

Principal sources of danger on board Ro-Ro vessels:

These can be classified into four broad areas:

- Ship related

- Cargo related

- Lashing and securing related

- Personnel related

Ship related dangers and means of preventing:

1. Poorly maintained ramps, lifts and bow and stern doors.
    Retractable car-decks, ramps and lifting appliances should be of sound construction, fitted with appropriate fencing and tested by a competent person. A planned maintenance system should be in operation.

2. Poorly maintained, inadequately illuminated or badly planned decks.
    Adequate permanent lighting should be provided to illuminate vehicle decks, ramps and lifting appliances. Lights are to be positioned so as to reduce to a minimum the shadow areas caused by stowed vehicles.

3. Wet decks.
    Adequate availability of equipment to deal with spillage i.e. drip trays or absorbent material. Decks to be kept as dry as possible.

4. Inadequate securing points.
    The ship should be provided with an adequate number of securing points of a sufficient strength. Enough cargo securing gear should be available,

as detailed in the vessel's Cargo Securing Manual. The duration of the voyage and the type of cargo must be taken into account when designing the securing arrangements.

<u>Cargo related dangers and means of preventing:</u>

1. The unsatisfactory condition or design of vehicles presented for shipment in terms of inadequate number of securing points, inadequate strength of the securing points, ineffective braking system.
    Pre load inspection should be carried out and systems must be in place to reject unsuitable cargo.

2. Cargo in freight containers or in trailers badly stowed.
    Container or vehicle packing certificates must be obtained and a pre-load inspection carried out where possible.

3. Free surface effect in tank vehicles and tank containers that are slack.
    Margins must be added to stability calculations for free surface effect when loading tank vehicles full of liquid.

4. Vehicles being moved negligently on vehicle decks and ramps.
    Adequate systems to be in place to prevent negligent movement of vehicles on decks and ramps.

5. Failure to apply the handbrakes.
    After loading, a nominated crewmember should check that the handbrakes are applied.

6. Excess free play in vehicle suspensions.
    This will affect lashings as they may come loose due to the movement of the vehicle suspensions in a seaway. In the case of air suspensions in larger vehicles, air is often drained out prior to lashing them.

7. Failure to comply with the IMDG code.
    Prior to loading vehicles or trailers with dangerous goods, a dangerous goods note and a vehicle packing certificate is needed. The goods must be stowed and segregated as per the IMDG code and only in spaces allowed by the vessel's Document of Compliance for loading dangerous goods.

<u>Lashing and securing related dangers</u>

Lashing and securing points must be adequate and the lashing material on board must be as per the vessels approved *Cargo Securing Manual*. The lashing plan must take into account the type and duration of the voyage and the lashings must be monitored and tightened at regular intervals. All securing must be completed before the vessel proceeds out to sea. Freight vehicles over 3.5 tonnes must be secured in all circumstances when expected conditions are such that movement of the vehicles relative to the ship can be expected. Lashings should not be released for unloading before the vessel is secured to the berth unless expressly ordered to do so by the Master. A planned maintenance system must be in place for the lashing equipment and adequate records must be available for inspection.

The movement, stowage and securing of vehicles must be under the close supervision of a responsible officer. Vehicles should be, so far as is possible, stowed in a fore and aft manner. Vehicles should not obstruct access to emergency escapes and bow and stern doors, and must not be stowed across water curtains.

Personnel related dangers and means of preventing:

1. Poor traffic management on and of the decks and ramps.
   The movement, storage and securing must be under the supervision of a responsible deck officer.

2. Risk of injury due to moving vehicles.
   Separating the means of access of passengers and vehicles should eliminate this. Supervisors must use clear and proper signals. All personnel engaged in the cargo operation should wear hi-visibility clothing and PPE. Passengers must not be allowed on vehicle decks prior to the safe berthing of the vessel. Clear markings and notices, warning of the dangers of remaining on vehicle decks, must be in place on pedestrian walkways

3. Slips, trips and falls.
   Decks must be kept free of oil and grease. Adequate illumination must be available at all times.

4. Risk of suffocation due to exhaust gasses
   Engines must be switched off as soon as possible and the ventilation system must be in operation at all times during cargo operation. The oxygen levels in the air must be continually monitored using fixed or portable indicators.

LIVERPOOL JOHN MOORES UNIVERSITY
LEARNING & INFORMATION SERVICES

REEFER CARGOES

KEY POINTS

- Reefer cargoes require special care due to their perishable nature
- Safe carriage depends on maintaining suitable storage conditions during transportation

---

Refrigerated cargoes include both frozen and chilled goods, the latter including fresh fruits and vegetables. Generally, frozen goods do not suffer if over-cooled, whereas chilled goods can be damaged by low temperatures, either by freezing or by chilling injury to the fresh produce. Many chilled cargoes are damaged if subjected to temperatures below that experienced in the growing area.

Successful transportation depends on the following factors:

- Shipper carriage instructions
- Crew knowledge of the refrigeration plant
- Preparation of hold spaces to the required standard
- Continuous monitoring of hold atmosphere

Shipper carriage instructions:

The responsibility for specifying carriage instructions belongs to the shipper, who is the owner of the goods. Only the shipper knows the full nature of the goods and their requirements. The exact nature of the cargo needs to be known - in the case of fruit, for example, carriage requirements may vary dependent on type, variety, maturity, origin and growing season conditions. Shipper's instructions should also specify the ventilation, stowage humidity and segregation needs.

Such carriage instructions should be supplied to the ship well in advance so that the crew can begin preparations in good time. On board record keeping is vital in case of reefer cargoes. This protects the ship-owner from expensive cargo damage claims and provides proof that the crew complied with the shippers instructions.

Types of refrigeration plants:

Types of refrigeration plant in common use are:

1.   DIRECT EXPANSION GRID COOLING

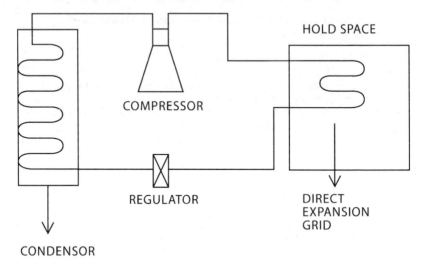

The refrigerant gas is compressed/ condensed and passed through a piping system that is attached to the bulkheads and deck heads of the cargo space. Heat is transferred to the coolant passing through the pipelines and is then led back to the refrigerant plant.

Advantages:

- Cheapest method of cooling chambers
- Cooling grids are fixed at the source of heat ingress
- Cooling can be continued throughout cargo operations

Disadvantages:

- Variations in grid temperatures due to ship movement
- Problems with leakage
- Frosting can occur on the grids
- May have problems fitting grids around holds & hatch covers
- Usually only commercially viable for a smaller ship

2. BRINE BATTERY COOLING SYSTEM

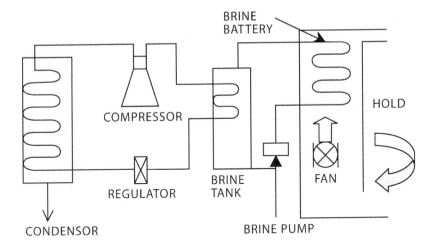

In this system brine[1] is cooled using a conventional refrigeration system and the cooled brine is then circulated, using the brine pump via fixed pipelines, around holds. Air is then blown across the cold brine and circulated through the hold. The salinity of the solution can be adjusted in order to lower the freezing point of the brine.

Advantages:

- No need to circulate expensive refrigerant gas throughout the holds.

- Easier to control temperature as less pipelines contain the refrigerant

- No possibility of gas leaks in the hold

- Brine is relatively inexpensive to replace in case of leaks

- Brine can be heated or cooled to allow for a range of temperatures.

Disadvantages:

- Expensive to install, with high capital costs.

- Air trunking is required in holds, which reduces cargo space

- Forced air is blown through the hold, which may dry the cargo.

- It cannot run while loading is in progress due to cold air blast inside the holds

---

[1] *Water saturated with or containing large amounts of a salt, especially sodium chloride or calcium chloride*

Hold Preparation

Reefer cargoes, being perishable in nature, require a great deal of care before loading and during carriage. Since most reefer cargoes are for human consumption, cleanliness of the compartments is of utmost importance.

The crew's understanding of the reefer plant is also important and pre-cooling checks should be carried out prior to operating the plant. The insulation must be checked for possible damage, the fans tested and the air ducting, sounding and scupper pipes must be checked. The actual process of cleaning the holds depends on the cargo to be loaded. Often the shipper specifies the standard of cleanliness required and may appoint a surveyor for a pre load inspection. The cleaning products to be used are sometimes prescribed by the shipping line and alternative products must not be used without permission.

In some cases a mere dry wipe and sweep may suffice although often a more thorough cleaning is required. This may be in case of changing cargoes from meat to fish or from frozen to chilled. In such cases the holds are washed down and wiped clean with cloths drenched in a disinfectant solution. The bilges are thoroughly cleaned and disinfected. The gratings are also removed and washed with a disinfectant solution. Bloodstains or other deposits must be scraped out as this can be a fertile breeding ground for bacteria. The hold may be sprayed using antiseptic spray to prevent the growth of bacteria and moulds.

Residual odours from previous cargoes must also be removed or cargoes will be spoiled by *taint*[2]. On dedicated reefer ships brine is pumped into the drainage pipes on tween decks. These pipes have an "S" bend and the brine remains standing in the bend. Since brine has a low freezing point it will not freeze nor allow odours to pass through the pipe while still allowing any drip water to flow to the bilges.

Any dunnage is inspected and unusable dunnage is disposed off. Air filled dunnage is increasingly used on modern ships because of environmental concerns about the disposal of untreated wood. If any hooks and chains are used in the transportation process they may need to be sterilised.

Once the hold is cleaned and dry then the *pre-cooling* process can begin. This usually takes about 48 hours. Any wooden dunnage to be used must be pre-cooled at the same time. All temperatures must be recorded in the *temperature log*. Once the hold is at the right temperature the surveyor usually inspects the hold and gives a survey report based on his findings. If the shipper accepts this then the loading process can begin.

---

[2] *Cargoes such as cheese are sensitive to taint and must be separated from strong smelling cargoes or cleaning material.*

Stowage and Cargo Care

Prior to loading the cargo it should be inspected for damage. The shipowner is not usually liable for any damage claims that are registered prior to loading.

Once the cargo is loaded on board then proper care must be exercised in the stowage process. "Live" cargoes need a supply of fresh air in order to survive and the stowage should be carefully monitored in order to avoid *shortcycling*.

Shortcycling is when a section of the cargo does not receive fresh air due to being stowed too close together. Since airflow chooses the path of least resistance it passes around rather than through the cargo. Dunnage can be used to prevent this from happening. Frozen cargoes usually require no ventilation and this should be checked. The carriage temperature requirements must be carefully noted and in particular the units must be checked. Although degrees Celsius are the international standard, in the USA degrees Fahrenheit is still commonly used. As zero° C is a common chilled goods temperature and zero° F is a common frozen goods temperature, great care is needed to avoid possible confusion of units.

Once the cargo is properly stowed the temperatures must be carefully monitored during the voyage. Accurate records must be maintained to avoid future cargo damage claims.

References:
"Refrigeration at Sea", (1978) Second Edition, Munton R & Stott JR, Applied Science Publishers, London
"Marine Refrigeration Manual" Capt. A.W.C Alders; 1987 Rotterdam Marine Chartering Agents

HAZARDS OF BULK CARGOES

KEY POINTS

- Bulk cargoes transported by sea have inherent hazards
- Knowledge of the hazards is important in order to safely transport these cargoes

The main hazards of bulk cargoes are as follows:

- Liquefaction
- Cargo shift
- Structural damage due to improper distribution
- Chemical hazards
- Other health hazards

Liquefaction:

Excessive moisture content in certain cargoes may cause the cargoes to liquefy due to the vibration caused by the ships movement. This can cause a *flow state* to develop, resulting in a loss of stability and structural damage due to impact. Compaction and vibration may cause a viscous fluid state to develop and the cargo may flow to one side of the ship with a roll one way but not completely return with a roll the other way. Thus the ship may progressively reach a dangerous heel and capsize.

Appendix A of the Bulk Cargo (BC) Code provides a list of such cargoes. At moisture content above that of the cargoes *transportable moisture limit (TML),* shift of cargo may occur as a result of liquefaction. In case of certain cargoes this can also occur below TML due to rapid *moisture migration*[1]. Such cargoes should be trimmed level and loaded as deep as is possible.

This moisture content in certain cargoes may be as a result of that cargoes' properties or because of the fact that many bulk cargoes are stowed in the open, without shelter. Cargoes affected include fine granular cargoes such as fine coal and concentrates.

---

[1] The movement of moisture from within the substance to the surface caused mainly by vibration.

Precautions as given in the *BC Code:*

- Ships other than specially constructed ships should only carry these cargoes if the moisture content does not exceed the TML, as defined in the code.

- Cargoes containing liquids should not be stowed in the same cargo space above or adjacent to consignments of cargoes with a tendency to liquefaction.

- Adequate precautions must be taken to prevent the entry of water into the holds.

- Whilst at sea, water should not be used as a cooling medium for such cargoes.

- Specially fitted cargo ships

    o If the moisture content exceeds the TML then such materials may be carried in cargo ships designed with portable divisions that contain any shift of cargo. Such divisions should be of sufficient strength and not constructed of wood.

    o Approval from the administration is required prior carrying such material in these ships

- Specially constructed cargo ships

    o Ships may be specially constructed to carry the above cargoes and will be approved to do so by their respective administrations.

Section 8 of the BC Code details test procedures for verifying the moisture content of cargoes. A simple shipboard test procedure as detailed in the BC Code is as follows:

> "Half fill a cylindrical can (0.5 to 1 ℓ) with a sample of the material, Strike a hard surface with the can sharply from a height of about 0.2 meters, repeating about 25 times at one or two second intervals. Examine the surface for free moisture or fluid conditions. If apparent then arrangements should be made to have additional laboratory tests conducted before the material is accepted for shipment."

Prior to loading such cargoes the Master should insist on a certificate from the shipper or the terminal, detailing the moisture content of a representative sample of the substance. Such a certificate will form a part of the information exchange between ship and terminal, as required by the *BLU Code.*

<u>Risk of cargo shift:</u>

A shift of cargo on passage may result if non-cohesive cargo is stowed incorrectly. The risk of cargoes shifting is determined by their *"angle of repose"*.

An angle of repose is defined as:
    "*..the maximum slope angle of non-cohesive i.e free flowing, granular material. It is the angle between the horizontal plane and the cone of such material when at rest on a plane surface.*"

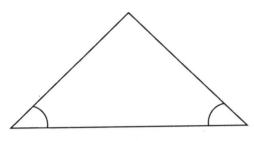

Angles of Repose

Cargoes with an angle of repose of less than 35 degrees are considered to be in danger of shifting. Cargoes with an angle of repose higher than 35 degrees have less likelihood of shifting due to the cohesive nature of such cargoes. In other words the *lesser* the angle of repose the *higher* the danger of a cargo shift.

A shipboard test to determine the angle of repose of a granular substance is detailed in the BC code appendix D.

To prevent a shift of cargo, in general, all bulk cargoes should be trimmed level and to the boundaries of the holds as far as is possible. At the very least all cargoes must be trimmed to well below the cargoes' angle of repose. In case of cargoes with a very low angle of repose (below 30 degrees), special precautions are needed and for such cargoes, which will be similar in nature to grain, the *International Grain Code* must be consulted and followed.[2]

<u>Structural hazards due to improper distribution:</u>

In recent years, due to increasing numbers of incidents involving casualties that are caused by structural damage, attention has focussed on this aspect of bulk carriers. SOLAS chapter XII "*Additional safety measures for bulk carriers*" addresses these concerns. In the UK, *SI 2151 of 2004* makes the fitting of water level detectors in holds, ballast tanks and void spaces and drainage and pumping systems compulsory. This is in line with SOLAS chapter XII 2004 amendments.

---

[2] *See the chapter on carriage of bulk grain.*

Structural damage to bulk carriers can occur because of excessive loading rates of high density cargo or due to such cargo being dropped into the hold from a height. The BLU code addresses these concerns and such items form a part of the ship-shore safety checklist on bulk carriers.

Structural damage to bulk carriers can also occur through improper weight distribution of the cargo. This can be caused by excessive concentration of weight in a particular area of the vessel. "*Alternate hold loading*" can cause excessive shearing forces and resultant stresses in the ships structure, as shown by the following diagram.

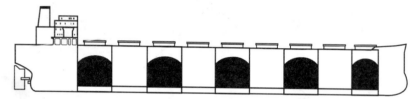

This sort of loading should only be allowed if the alternate holds are specially strengthened. The advantage of loading alternate holds is that it raises the centre of gravity and eases racking stresses.

"*Block hold loading*" where cargo is stowed in blocks of two or more adjoining holds should only be adopted when either such a loading condition is described in the approved loading manual or approved local loading criteria defines the maximum weight limit in each hold or block of holds as a function of the ships mean draught

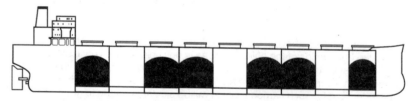

Uneven distribution of the cargo throughout the vessel's length can cause excessive shearing forces and bending moments. Prior to loading, a cargo plan must be made and due allowance must be made for the rates of ballast discharge. The BLU code details a pro forma loading plan.[3] A *Loadicator* is normally used to ensure that the stresses on the ship do not exceed set limits.

Improper distribution of weight can lead to excessive stability, especially with high-density cargoes such as iron ore. This can result in *raking stresses* on the ship structure. The resulting heavy rolling caused by excessive stability can also cause a shift of cargo.

---

[3] *See the chapter on the BLU Code.*

Chemical and Other Health Hazards

Some bulk cargoes, like sulphur, are hazardous to human health because of their toxic or corrosive nature. Such cargoes are listed in Appendix B of the BC Code[4]. Some of these materials are classified as dangerous goods in the International Maritime Dangerous Goods Code (IMDG Code), others are materials which may cause hazards when transported in bulk. Such material must be carefully segregated from other materials.

Hazards from such cargoes include the possibility of a flammable atmosphere being created, for example methane emission in coal, toxicity, corrosive properties, irritant dust, or oxygen depletion.

Prior to loading cargoes that have chemical hazards it is important that adequate information is obtained from the shipper. This information should list all known chemical hazards of the cargo and the precautions to be taken on board. Such precautions will include, among other things, proper PPE to be worn, atmosphere tests, no smoking regulations enforced, proper cargo venting precautions, protecting machinery from cargo dust, wearing of dust masks, and securing of all openings to the accommodation. *SI 336 Carriage of Cargoes* regulation makes it mandatory on UK registered vessels to carry atmosphere-monitoring equipment on board, together with training and instructions for its use.

---

[4] *See the chapter on BC code for further information*

BC CODE – CODE OF SAFE PRACTICE FOR SOLID BULK CARGOES

KEY POINTS

- Chapter VI of SOLAS recommends an internationally acceptable code of safe practice for the carriage of solid bulk cargoes.

- The BC Code provides guidance to administrations, ship owners, shippers and masters to the safe stowage and shipment of solid bulk cargoes, excluding grain.

- It is mandatory for UK flagged ships, and other ships, when in UK waters, to carry a copy of this code on board, as per "*SI 336: Carriage of Cargoes Regulations, 1999*"

What is it for?

It gives guidance on the standards to be applied in the safe stowage and shipment of solid bulk cargoes *excluding* grain.

It includes general advice on the procedures to be followed whenever bulk cargoes are shipped, a description of the hazards associated with certain materials, lists of typical bulk materials and recommended test procedures to determine the various characteristics of solid bulk cargoes. The BC Code deals with three basic types of cargo:

BC Code

Code of Safe
Practice for
Solid Bulk Cargoes

- Those which may liquefy,

- Materials which possess chemical hazards

- Materials which fall into neither of these categories but may nevertheless pose other dangers.

The Code highlights the dangers associated with the shipment of certain types of bulk cargoes, gives guidance on various procedures that should be adopted, lists typical products that are shipped in bulk, gives advice on their properties and how they should be handled and describes various test procedures that should be employed to determine the characteristic cargo properties.

<u>Contents of the code</u>

Introduction: A list of hazards associated with the shipment of materials

- Structural damage due to improper distribution
- Loss or reduction of stability during the voyage
    - Due to cargo shift
    - Due to liquefaction
- Chemical Reactions

Section 1 : contains key definitions related to bulk cargoes including angle of repose, flow state, etc. [1]

Section 2 : which deals with general precautions

Cargo distribution

- Guidance to prevent the structure from becoming overstressed.
- For high-density materials, the maximum number of tonnes loaded in any cargo space should not exceed *0.9 LBD tonnes (L = length of hold, B = average breadth of hold, D = summer draught).*
- If material is trimmed level then the maximum tonnes loaded in the lower hold can be increased by 20%.
- For untrimmed or partially trimmed material, the corresponding height of material pile peak above the cargo space floor should not exceed 1.1 x D x Stowage factor.
- Master to be provided with adequate information about the material to be shipped by the shipper, e.g. stowage factor, history of shifting, any particular problems and information to aid in stability calculations on board.

Loading and unloading

- Prepare cargo spaces prior loading
- Make sure bilge lines, sounding pipes, bilge fittings etc are in order
- Sound bilges after completion of loading
- Protect sensitive navigation equipment and deck machinery from dust, shutdown ventilation systems and put accommodation air-conditioning system on recirculation.

---

[1] Refer to the chapter "*Hazards of bulk cargoes.*"

Section 3: which deals with the safety of the personnel and the ship

- General requirements
- Poisoning, corrosive and asphyxiation hazards
    - o Shipper should inform about any chemical hazards
    - o Master should take all necessary precautions, including those for oxygen depletion and toxic gases
    - o Precautions to be followed for entry into enclosed spaces
- Health hazards due to dust
- Flammable atmosphere caused by fine dust and flammable gases emitted by cargoes
- Advice on Ventilation
- Precaution for grain in in-transit fumigation
    - o Should be as per the latest version of the "*Recommendation on the safe use of pesticides in ships.*"

Section 4 : which provides an assessment of acceptability for safe shipment

- The shipper should provide details about the material being shipped prior to shipment. These should include among the following:
    - o Chemical hazards
    - o Flow moisture point
    - o Stowage factor
    - o Moisture content
    - o Angle of repose
- The shipper will arrange tests to be carried out on the material and certificates of test should be obtained. As examples:
    - o Moisture content: certificates containing the TML should be accompanied by a statement stating that the moisture content is the average moisture content at the time of shipment.
    - o Chemical hazards
- The Master should ensure that such certificates are handed over to him prior to shipment.

Section 5: Trimming Procedures

- To minimise the dangers of a cargo shift the cargo should be trimmed reasonably level to the boundaries of the hold.

- Documented history of the cargo should be made available to provide an indication of the cargo behaviour in the past.

Section 6: Methods of determining the angle of repose

Shipboard test to determine angle of repose.[2]

Section 7: Cargoes which may liquefy

Properties, characteristics and hazards of cargoes that may liquefy

- Appendix A to the code contains a list of such cargoes

- At moisture content above that of the TML, shift of cargo may occur as a result of liquefaction.

- In case of certain cargoes this can also occur below TML because of rapid moisture migration.

- Such cargoes should be trimmed level and loaded as deep as is possible.

- Compaction and vibration may cause a viscous fluid state to develop and the cargo may flow to one side of the ship with a roll one way but not completely return with a roll the other way. Thus the ship may progressively reach a dangerous heel and capsize.

Precautions

- Ships, other than specially constructed ships, should only carry these cargoes if the moisture content does not exceed the TML, as defined in the code.

- Cargoes containing liquids should not be stowed in the same cargo space above or adjacent to consignments of such cargoes.

- Adequate precautions must be taken to prevent the entry of water into the holds.

- Whilst at sea, water should not be used as a cooling medium for such cargoes.

---

[2] Refer to *"Hazards of bulk cargoes."*

Specially fitted cargo ships

- If the moisture content exceeds the TML then such materials may be carried in cargo ships designed with portable divisions that contain any shift of cargo. Such divisions should be of sufficient strength and not constructed of wood.

- Approval from the administration is required prior to carrying such material in these ships.

- Ships may be specially constructed to carry the above cargoes and will be approved to do so by their respective administrations.

Section 8: Test procedures for cargoes that may liquefy.

Shipboard test to determine risk of liquefaction.[3]

Section 9: Materials possessing chemical hazards

Such materials may be materials classified as dangerous goods as per the IMDG code or materials hazardous only in bulk (MHB). Such materials are listed in appendix B of the code.

- Master should obtain currently valid information about the physical and chemical properties of the cargoes to be transported.

- Approval from the concerned competent authorities should be obtained for the transport of hazardous materials not listed in appendix B.

- Classification of materials possessing chemical hazards and intending to be shipped in bulk is in accordance with the IMDG code.

- Materials hazards only in bulk (MHB) are defined as "materials, when carried in bulk, possess sufficient hazards to require specific precautions". For example materials liable to self heat or reduce oxygen in the space.

Stowage and segregation requirements

- The table lists the segregation of bulk materials possessing chemical hazards and dangerous goods that are carried in packaged form.

- Segregation between incompatible bulk materials possessing chemical hazards qualities is listed in the table.

---

[3] Refer to *"Hazards of bulk cargoes."*

Section 10: Transport of solid bulk wastes

This section outlines the requirements for the transport of solid wastes in bulk.

- Wastes are defined as solid materials containing or contaminated with materials possessing chemical hazards and which are carried for dumping or incineration

- In addition to the documentation required for solid bulk material, a waste movement document should be carried for all trans-boundary movements of waste.

- Waste should be classified as per the chemical hazards it possesses and segregated according to the code

- In the event of an incident involving these goods, which may constitute a danger for the ship or the environment, the competent authorities of the countries of origin and destination should be informed and their advice obtained.

Appendix A – List of bulk materials which may liquefy

This lists materials that may liquefy if carried at moisture content in excess of the transportable moisture limit.

Appendix B – List of bulk material possessing chemical hazards

This lists materials that are known to have chemical hazards that may give rise to a dangerous situation on board.

The materials are listed along with their UN numbers, IMO class, EmS no., properties, observations, stowage and segregation requirements and any special requirements.

Some of the classified materials listed also appear in the International Maritime Dangerous Goods (IMDG) Code when carried in packaged form, but others become hazardous only when they are carried in bulk - for example, because they might reduce the oxygen content of a cargo space or are prone to self-heating. Examples are woodchips and coal.

Appendix B

SILICOMANGANESE*
(With known hazard profile or known to evolve gases)
With a silicon content of 25% or more

BC No.	IMO class	MFAG table no.	Approximate Stowage Factor (m³/t)	EmS NO.
060	MHB	601,605	0.18 to 0.26	B2

Properties
In contact with water, alkalis or acids may evolve hydrogen, a flammable gas; may also produce phosphine and arsine, which are highly toxic gases.

Observations
Prior to loading, a certificate should be provided by the manufacturer or shipper stating that, after manufacture, the material was stored under cover, but exposed to the open air for not less than three days prior to shipment.

Segregation and stowage requirements
Segregation as required for class 4.3 materials.
"Separated from" foodstuffs and all class 8 liquids.
Only to be loaded under dry weather conditions.
Keep dry.
To be stowed in a mechanically ventilated space.

Special requirements
Ventilation should be such that any escaping gases cannot reach living quarters on or under deck.

Appendix C – Lists bulk materials that are neither liable to liquefy nor to possess chemical hazards.

The materials are listed in a tabular form with their approximate angle of repose, stowage factor and properties, observations and special requirements.

Appendix D – Lists the laboratory test procedures, associated apparatus and standards.

This also lists a shipboard test method to determine the angle of repose using a protractor.

Appendix E – Lists the Emergency Schedules (EmS) for materials possessing chemical hazards that are listed in appendix B.

EMERGENCY SCHEDULE B2

ALUMINIUM FERROSILICON POWDER (UN No. 1395)
ALUMINIUM SILICON POWDER, UNCOATED (UN No. 1398)
FERROPHOSPHORUS (BC No. 020)
FERRO SILICON (UN No. 1408) (BC No. 022)
SILICOMANGANESE (BC No. 060)

Special emergency equipment to be carried

Self-contained breathing apparatus

EMERGENCY PROCEDURES

Wear self-contained breathing apparatus.

EMERGENCY ACTION IN A FIRE SITUATION

Batten down and use CO_2 if available, **Do not use water**.

Medical first aid

UN/BC no.	Material	MFAG table no.
1395	ALUMINIUM FERROSILICON	601 and 605
1398	ALUMINIUM SILICON	NONE
BC 020	FERROPHOSPHORUS	601 and 605
1408, BC 022	FERRO SILICON	601 and 605
BC 060	SILICOMANGANESE	NONE

Remarks: Materials are virtually non-combustible when dry

This section also advises the carriage of additional protective clothing, Breathing Apparatus (BA) sets, and spray jets for dealing with emergencies involving bulk solids.

The emergency action described in the code is mainly for use at sea.

In general the best action is to batten down the hold and exclude all air from the cargo space. There are notable exceptions to this rule e.g. ammonium nitrate fertilisers.

The Medical first aid advice refers to the "Medical first aid guide for use in accidents involving dangerous goods (MFAG)".

Appendix F – Lists recommendations for entering enclosed spaces aboard ships

This lists precautions for the assessment of risks, permit to work systems, testing the atmosphere and precautions during entry. A sample permit to work checklist is attached.

This section also lists oxygen depleting cargoes and materials that may be carried in bulk.

Appendix G – Procedures for gas monitoring of coal cargoes

This lists sampling, measurement and observation procedures for coal cargoes carried in bulk.

BLU CODE

KEY POINTS

- IMO published the BLU code in response to increasing losses of bulk carriers

- Gives guidance to terminals and vessels for the safe loading and unloading of bulk carriers

The '*Code of practice for the safe loading and unloading of bulk carriers' (BLU Code)* was written in response to continued losses of ships carrying solid bulk cargoes. This code provides guidance to masters of bulk carriers, terminal operators and other parties concerned with the safe handling, loading and unloading of solid bulk cargoes.

BLU Code

For UK flag vessels and other vessels in UK waters the contents of the code are mandatory with effect from the 1st of March 2004, vide the "*Merchant Shipping (Safe Loading and Unloading of Bulk Carriers) Regulations 2003*".

Contents of the code are as follows:

Definitions of terms

- Air draught

- Combination carrier

- Conveyer system

- Trimming

Suitability of Ships and Terminals

Ships are required to carry:

- Valid certification

- Stability and loading booklets

- Stress calculators and be suitable for the intended cargo.

Terminals to have:

- Equipment certification
- Calibrated weighing equipment
- Knowledge of the hazards of bulk cargoes
- Trained and rested personnel and only accept ships that can safely berth alongside their installation.

Procedures Between Ship and Terminal Prior to Arrival

Information exchange

- Loading rates
- Cargo handling plan
- Air draught; draught
- Cargo properties
- Limitations on loading procedures and cargo details
- Trimming procedures

Procedures for cargo loading

- Completion of safety checklist
- Loading rates
- Ballast rates
- Times for checking draught
- Stress limitations for ship's hull
- Communication procedures
- Accurate weight meters to within 1% of the intended accuracy
- Emergency procedures

Cargo Unloading and Handling of Ballast

- Avoid excessive stresses
- Unloading rates
- Inform terminal immediately in event of damage to ship
- Ship kept upright
- Communication arrangements

- On completion of unloading the master and the terminal representative should agree in writing that the ship has been unloaded in accordance with the agreed unloading plan, with the holds emptied and cleaned to the Master's requirements. Any detected damage suffered by the ship should be recorded.

Appendices

- Recommended contents of terminal information books
- Format for loading/unloading plan, with examples
- Ship/shore Safety Checklist and guidelines for completion
- Form for receiving cargo information containing items such as:
    - Stowage factor
    - Angle of repose
    - Trimming procedures
    - Moisture content
    - Transportable moisture limit
    - Chemical properties
    - Additional certificates to be attached for moisture content

LOADING AND CARRIAGE OF BULK COAL

KEY POINTS

- Coal is an inherently hazardous cargo carried commonly in bulk carriers.

- MGN 60 and the BC Code draws attention to the hazards of coal carriage and the precautions to be taken for the safe transport of coal cargoes.

The different types of coal that may be carried by sea include:

ANTHRACITE: Coal of a high rank which has a high carbon and low volatile matter content.

STEAM COAL: Bituminous coal normally used as fuel for power plants.

DUFF: Small, ungraded coal with a nominal upper size, usually below 10mm.

SIZED COAL: Graded coal containing a minimum amount of fines, suitable for domestic or industrial use.

WASHED COAL: Coal from which impurities have been reduced in order to improve its quality.

BUNKERING COAL: The supply of coal to bunkers for the bunkering of ships.

Hazards of coal cargoes include the following:

1. They may emit flammable gasses

    Coal cargoes may emit methane gas, which is flammable and lighter than air. The flammable range of methane is within the limits 5% to 16% and this mixture can ignite on the introduction of a source of ignition. Accumulations of this gas may take place between the hatch coamings and the top of the cargo.

    Methane may also leak into adjacent places and adjoining tanks. To prevent against this MGN 60 and the BC code recommend surface ventilating the hold for 24 hours after departure from the loading port. If the methane concentration is found to be acceptably low at the end of this period the ventilation should be stopped. On the other hand, if the concentration of methane as measured is over 20% of the LEL (Lower Explosive Limit), adequate surface ventilation is to be maintained to reduce the concentration.

    Smoking and naked flames should not be allowed within the vicinity of any coal cargoes and a hot work permit system must be in place.

2. It has a tendency to self heat

Some coals have a tendency to self heat and if this is the case the Shipper should be able to inform you prior to loading. Any self-heating is indicated by increasing concentration of carbon monoxide in the hold. To minimise the tendency of the coal to self heat MGN 60 recommends that the hatches are kept closed and surface ventilation is limited to the absolute minimum to remove any accumulated methane.

The BC Code also recommends that the cargo is trimmed level to avoid the formation of any gas pockets and to prevent air from entering the body of the coal, which may cause self heating. Carbon Monoxide may be produced as a by product of combustion. This is a toxic, odourless and flammable gas. The ship should also have available adequate instruments to detect and measure concentrations of harmful gases (methane, oxygen and carbon monoxide) within the hold. There should also be adequate sampling points sited as per appendix G of the BC Code.

Carbon monoxide, and where necessary temperature levels, shall be monitored at regular intervals and logged. If at the time of loading, when the hatches are open, the temperature of the coal exceeds 55°C, expert advice should be obtained prior to loading.

If the carbon monoxide level is increasing steadily, a potential self-heating may be developing. The cargo space should be completely closed down and all ventilation ceased. The master should seek expert advice immediately. Water should not be used for cooling the material or fighting coal cargo fires at sea, but may be used for cooling the boundaries of the cargo space

3. Oxidation

Coals may be subject to oxidation, which can result in the depletion of oxygen from the holds. This can be hazardous if proper precaution is not taken while entering spaces that may be lacking in oxygen. There should be adequate procedures in place for enclosed space entry and readings for oxygen must be taken prior to entry.

4. Reaction with water

Some coals are liable to react with water and produce acids that can cause corrosion. Flammable and toxic gases, including hydrogen, may be produced. Hydrogen is a colourless and odourless gas that is highly flammable and lighter than air.

Monitoring of bilge water for acidity levels using Ph indicator strips will give an indication of this happening and adequate precautions should be then taken to prevent a hazard from developing.

5. Liquefaction hazards.

If fine coals with a size of less than 7mm are carried there is a risk of the coal liquefying if the moisture content exceeds the *transportable moisture limit (TML)*. The Master should ensure that the moisture content does not exceed the TML and, if necessary, the onboard test as recommended in the BC Code is carried out to check the actual moisture content.

The BC code recommends the following precautions to be taken prior to loading, during carriage and discharge of all coal cargoes:

Prior to loading, the shipper or his appointed agent should provide, in writing to the master, the characteristics of the cargo and the recommended safe handling procedures for loading and transport of the cargo. As a minimum, the cargo's contract specifications for moisture content, sulphur content and size should be stated. It is important to state whether the cargo may be liable to emit methane or self-heat. The master should be satisfied that he has received such information prior to accepting the cargo. If the shipper has advised that the cargo is liable to emit methane or self-heat, the master should take the appropriate steps to prevent a hazard from developing.

Before and during loading, and while the material remains on board, the master should ensure the following:

- All cargo spaces and bilge wells should be clean and dry

- Any residue of waste material or previous cargo should be removed, including removable cargo battens, before loading.

- All electrical cables and components situated in cargo spaces and adjacent spaces should be free from defects. Such cables and electrical components should either be safe for use in an explosive atmosphere or they should be positively isolated.

- The ship should be suitably fitted and carry on board appropriate calibrated instruments for measuring concentrations of methane, oxygen and carbon monoxide and the pH value of cargo hold bilge samples. This should be possible without entering the space.

- Means should be provided for measuring the temperature of the cargo in the range 0°C to 100°C. Such arrangements should enable the temperature of the coal to be measured while being loaded and during the voyage without requiring entry into the cargo space.

- The ship should carry on board the self-contained breathing apparatus required by SOLAS regulation II/2 - 17. No smoking regulations must be imposed and warning signs and placards must be displayed.

- The master should ensure that the coal cargo is not stowed adjacent to hot areas.

Prior to departure, the master should be satisfied that the surface of the material has been trimmed reasonably level to the boundaries of the cargo space to avoid the formation of gas pockets and to prevent air from permeating the body of the coal. Casings leading into the cargo space should be adequately sealed. The shipper must ensure that the loading terminal cooperates with the ship during the loading process.

If the behaviour of the cargo during the voyage differs from that specified in the cargo declaration, the master should report such differences to the shipper. Such reports will enable the shipper to maintain records on the behaviour of the coal cargoes, so that in future the information provided to the master can be reviewed in the light of prior experience.

CARRIAGE OF BULK GRAIN

KEY POINTS

- Carriage of grain in bulk is hazardous due to the possibility of shift of cargo because of the low 'angle of repose' of grain

- "*International code for the safe carriage of grain in bulk*" details the principles and procedures for the safe carriage of grain

---

Compliance with the *International Grain Code* is a requirement under SOLAS. For UK ships and foreign flag ships in UK waters this is enforced by SI 336 (Carriage of cargoes regulations).

The "*International code for the safe carriage of grain in bulk*" normally applies to all ships, regardless of size, engaged in the transport of bulk grain. However, some ships may be exempted from complying with the Code by their flag state due to the sheltered nature of their trade or the specific conditions of the voyage.

Part A contains special requirements and gives guidance on the stowage of grain and the use of grain fittings.

Part B deals with the calculation of heeling moments and general assumptions.

Part C of the revised SOLAS Chapter VI, Regulation 9, stipulates the requirements for cargo ships carrying grain. This states that a cargo ship carrying grain shall comply with the requirements of the International Grain Code and hold a document of authorization as required by that Code. In Regulation 9.2, a ship without a document of authorization shall not load grain until the master satisfies the Contracting Governments of the port of loading that the ship complies with the requirements of the Code.

According to the Code the term *grain* covers the following cargoes:

"*...wheat, maize (corn), oats, rye, barley, rice, pulses, seeds and processed forms thereof, whose behaviour is similar to grain in its natural state.*"

In order to prove compliance with the Code a "*Document of Authorisation*" is issued for every ship that satisfies the conditions. This document should accompany or be incorporated into a ship specific "*grain loading manual*". Both these documents are issued by or approved on behalf of that ships flag state administration. A ship without a Document of Authorisation may be granted an *exemption* provided the Master can demonstrate compliance with the terms of the Code.

Contents of the grain-loading manual:

- Ships Particulars

- Light ship displacement

- Table of liquid free surface corrections

- Capacities and centres of gravity

- Curve or table of angle of flooding where less than 40°

- Curves or tables of hydrostatic properties, suitable for a range of operating draughts.

- Approved curves or tables of volumes, vertical centres of volumes and assumed volumetric heeling moments for every compartment.

- Approved tables or curves of maximum permissible heeling moments for varying displacements and varying vertical centres of gravity.

- Loading instructions

- A worked example, for the guidance of the Master.

- Loaded departure and arrival conditions for 3 representative stowage factors.

Stability Requirements

- Vessels should be able to demonstrate by calculations that at all times during the intended voyage the ship will have sufficient intact stability to provide adequate residual dynamic stability after taking into account the adverse heeling effect caused by an *assumed* shift of grain.

- The vessel should demonstrate by calculations that the maximum list will not be greater than 12° after experiencing

  o A shift of cargo of 15° in every FULL hold

  o A shift of cargo of 25° in any partly filled compartment.

- Net residual area between heeling arm curve and righting arm curve up to 40° (or angle of flooding if less than 40°) to be not less than 0.075 metre-radians.

- Initial metacentric height after free surface correction not to be less than 0.3 metres

- As many compartments full as possible

- Cargo to be trimmed level

Optional stability requirements for ships without a Document of Authorisation carrying partial cargoes of bulk grain:

The vessel may load grain if all the following conditions are met:

- Total weight of grain does not exceed one-third of the ship's deadweight

- Filled compartments, trimmed and fitted with centre line divisions extending, full length and to a maximum depth of 2.4m OR be saucered (except in case of linseed or other such seeds).

- Free grain surfaces in partially filled compartments to be trimmed level and secured in accordance with the code

- Must use GM 0.30 metres or as given by the formula in the code (Section A 9.1.5), whichever is greater.

- The Master must demonstrate to the administration that the ship, when loaded, will satisfy the requirements of this section of the code

Securing methods

In order to prevent a shift of cargo causing a heel beyond the permitted limits the code specifies methods of securing in full and partially full compartments.

In full compartments:

- Longitudinal shifting boards from the deckhead extending below the surface of the cargo

- For the purpose of reducing the heeling moment a saucer may be used in place of a longitudinal division. The depth of the saucer, measured from the bottom of the saucer to the deck line shall be as follows:

  o For ships with a moulded breadth of up to 9.1 mtrs not less than 1.2 mtrs, between 18.3m or more, not less than 1.8 m and others on interpolation.

  o The top of the saucer shall be formed by the under deck structure in way of the hatchway. The saucer and the hatchway above shall be completely filled with bagged grain or other suitable cargo laid down on a separation cloth and stowed tightly against the adjacent structure.

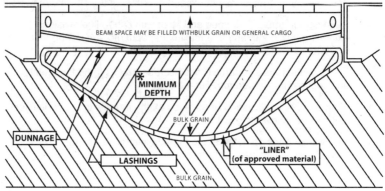

SAUCER SECURED BY "BUNDLING OF BULK"

0   BEAM SPACE MAY BE FILLED WITHBULK GRAIN OR GENERAL CARGO   0

MINIMUM DEPTH

BULK GRAIN

DUNNAGE

LASHINGS

"LINER" (of approved material)

BULK GRAIN

*MINIMUM DEPTH OF SAUCER IN A "FILLED COMPARTMENT"

Vessels with a moulded breadth up to 9.1m   =1.2m
Vessels with a moulded breadth 18.3m or more   =1.8m
(Interpolate for breadths between 9.1m and 18.3m)

Bundling: As an alternative to filling the saucer with bagged grain, a bundle of bulk grain may be used provided that the dimensions and the securing means are as given in the code.

Partly filled compartments:

- Overstowing the leveled off surface of the bulk grain with bagged grain on top of a separation cloth or a platform.

- Strapping or lashing two solid floors of lumber over the slightly crowned surface of the grain after covering with burlap or tarpaulin.

- Securing with a wire mesh, retained by wooden planks in place of the lumber pieces.

All lashings in partly filled compartments must be inspected regularly and tightened as necessary.

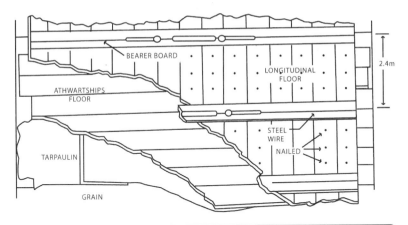

BEARER BOARD

LONGITUDINAL FLOOR

2.4m

ATHWARTSHIPS FLOOR

STEEL WIRE

NAILED

TARPAULIN

GRAIN

SECURING OF A "PARTLY FILLED" COMPARTMENT BY STRAPPING OR LASHING

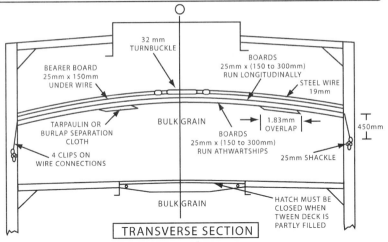

32 mm TURNBUCKLE

BOARDS
25mm x (150 to 300mm)
RUN LONGITUDINALLY

BEARER BOARD
25mm x 150mm
UNDER WIRE

STEEL WIRE
19mm

TARPAULIN OR
BURLAP SEPARATION
CLOTH

BULK GRAIN

1.83mm OVERLAP

450mm

BOARDS
25mm x (150 to 300mm)
RUN ATHWARTSHIPS

4 CLIPS ON
WIRE CONNECTIONS

25mm SHACKLE

BULK GRAIN

HATCH MUST BE
CLOSED WHEN
TWEEN DECK IS
PARTLY FILLED

TRANSVERSE SECTION

Prior to loading a cargo of grain, all holds must be thoroughly washed, dried and all residues of previous cargoes removed. Surveyors, appointed by shippers' prior to loading the cargo, may inspect the hold. Spaces should be closely inspected for insect infestation and fumigated if required. Any fumigation should be carried out in accordance with the IMO "*Recommendations on the safe use of pesticides in ships*" and MGN 284 –" *Recommendations for ships carrying fumigated bulk cargoes*".

CARRIAGE OF DANGEROUS GOODS

KEY POINTS

- Carriage of dangerous goods by sea is regulated by SOLAS and MARPOL

- The International Maritime Dangerous Goods Code (IMDG Code) is the legal framework for maritime transport of dangerous goods.

There are comprehensive and specific requirements surrounding the transport of dangerous goods at sea. The purpose of these requirements is to effectively protect the lives of seafarers, the safety of vessels and the maritime environment.

Dangerous Goods are divided into 9 classes based on their associated risks when transported by land, sea or air. This classification is based on UN recommendations made in 1957.

The various classes are:

Class 1   Explosives
Class 2   Gases
Class 3   Flammable Liquids
Class 4   Flammable Solids
            Substances liable to Spontaneous Combustion
            Substances, which in Contact with Water, emit Flammable Gas
Class 5   Oxidising Substances and Organic Peroxides
Class 6   Toxic and Infectious Substances
Class 7   Radioactive Material
Class 8   Corrosive Substances
Class 9   Miscellaneous Dangerous Substances

Documentation required prior loading

The regulations governing the carriage of dangerous goods by sea casts a responsibility on the *shipper* of the goods to provide "*Dangerous goods declaration*"[1]. This should include the following details:

a.   *The Proper Shipping Name of the material carried*
     This is not the trade name but can be the technical name, as long as it accurately describes the goods.

b.   *The UN Number*
     This is a 4 digit unique number allocated to all dangerous goods assigned by the United Nations committee of experts (UN List)

---

[1] *Also called as a "Dangerous Goods Note"*

c.   *Hazard class*
From 1 to 9 as elaborated above

d.   *Packing Group (when assigned)*
Dangerous substances of Classes 3, 4, 5, 6,1 and 8 have been assigned to one of three categories (Packaging Groups), according to the degree of danger they present:

- Great danger-Packaging Group I (PGI)

- Medium danger-Packaging Group II (PGII)

- Minor danger-Packaging Group III (PGIII)

The greater the degree of danger, the more stringent the packaging requirement will be. For other classes packaging groups may be assigned depending on the degree of severity of any leakage of the substance.

For the Sequence of the Information, two options are allowed:

a, b, c, d OR

b, c, a, d

Examples

> *"UN1098 ALLYL ALCOHOL, 6.1 (3), I"*
> *"ALLYL ALCOHOL, 6.1 (3), UN1098, I"*

e.   *Subsidiary Risk*
This is an additional risk that may be present in certain goods. For example, a corrosive substance may also be flammable.

f.   *Marine Pollutant*
This classification is included for any substance so classified as per Annex 3 of MARPOL.

g.   *Number of Packages*
Total number of packages to be transported as a unit.

h.   *Total Quantities*
The total volume or mass (in kilograms) is stated for each item of dangerous goods bearing a different Proper Shipping Name. For Class 1 goods the quantity shall be the net explosive mass.

If the dangerous goods are transported according to the exceptions for dangerous goods packed in limited quantities,[2] then the words "Limited Quantities" shall be included.

---

[2] *Column 7 of the DG list, IMDG Code Volume 2*

i. *Flashpoint*
    If applicable, for liquid dangerous substances the flashpoint shall be included.

j. *Any other information required by the IMDG Code or local regulations.*
    This will include additional information such as the 24 hour emergency contact number required for shipments to the US and additional certificates such as a weathering certificate, etc.

k. *Container/Vehicle Packing Certificate*
    When dangerous goods are packed or loaded into any container or vehicle, those responsible for packing the container or vehicle shall provide a "container/vehicle packing certificate" specifying the container/vehicle identification number and certifying that the operation is carried out in accordance with the following conditions:

    - The container is clean and dry and fit to receive the goods

    - Packaging and labelling is carried out as per the IMDG Code

    - Segregation within the Container/Vehicle is as per the IMDG Code

    - Container is marked & labelled as per the IMDG Code

    - A DG note *(on next page)* has been received for each dangerous goods consignment loaded in the container/vehicle.

The container/vehicle packing certificate and declaration serves a separate function to the dangerous goods declaration, and different people very often sign the two. However, for the sake of convenience the two declarations are often included in the same document.

DANGEROUS GOODS NOTE

Exporter	1	Customs reference/status	2
BATHUNT (UK) PLC PO BOX 830 CROYDON SURREY CR9 9NZ		3GB 214832591000-T63981	

	Booking number	3	Exporter's reference	4
	BN001251		T6-3981	

	Forwarder's reference	5
	ARG 4367H	

Consignee	6	DSHA Notification/in accordance with DSHA regulations (as ammended) given by	6A

CASILLA BOX S.A. CASILLA DE CORRERO 6091 BUENOS AIRES ARGENTINA		Shipper	Cargo Agent	Transport operator	Shipping line
			X		

Freight forwarder	7	International carrier	8
FORREST FORWARD COMPANY VENTURA BUSINESS PARK STAFFORDSHIRE DE15 4ZY		ORCHARD SHIPPING	
		For use of receiving authority only	

Other UK transport details (e.g. ICD, terminal, vehicle bkg. ref. receiving dates	9
DELIVER TO CONTAINERBASE MANCHESTER BY 5/6/03	

		I hereby declare that the contents of this consignment are fully and accurately described below by proper shipping name, and are classified, packaged, marked and labelled/placarded and are in all respects in proper condition for transport according to the applicable international and national governmental regulations and in accordance with the provisions shown overleaf. The shipper must complete and sign box 17	10A

Vessel	Port of loading	10
ORCHARD EMPRESS	LIVERPOOL	

Port of Discharge	Destination	11	TO THE RECEIVING AUTHORITY- Please receive for shipment the goods described below subject to your published regulations and conditions (including those as to liability)
BUENOS AIRES			

Shipping marks SPECIFY: Proper Shipping Name*. Hazard Class, UN No Additional Information (if applicable) see overleaf For RID/ ADR/ CDG Road requirements see notes overleaf	Number and kind of packages; description of goods	12	Net weight (kg) of goods	13	Gross weight (kg) of goods	13A	Cube (m ³) (kg) of goods	14
CB 11821 BUENOS AIRES UN 1098 ALLYL ALCOHOL, 6.1(3), I	1 PALLET CONTAINING 10X200L DRUMS ALLYL ALCOHOL		1,800		2,000		4.00	

* Proper Shipping Name - Trade names alone are unacceptable

CONTAINER/VEHICLE **PACKING CERTIFICATE** I hereby declare that the goods described above have been packed/ loaded into the container vehicle identified below in accordance with the provisions shown overleaf. THE DECLARATION MUST BE COMPLETED AND SIGNED FOR ALL CONTAINER/ VEHICLE LOADS BY THE PERSON RESPONSIBLE FOR PACKING/LOADING	Name of Company Name/ Status of Declarant Place and date Signature of Declarant	THIS BOX WOULD BE COMPLETED BY THE COMPANY RESPONSIBLE FOR LOADING THE CONTAINER	Total gross weight of goods 2,000	Total cube of goods 4.00

Container identification number/ vehicle registration number	15	Seal number(s)		15A	Container/ vehicle size and type	15B	Tare (kg)	15C	Total gross weight (including tare) (kg)	15D
STPU284152/5		238795			40' GENERAL STANDARD HEIGHT		2,500		4,500	

HAULIER DETAILS	**DOCK/TERMINAL RECIEPT** RECEIVING AUTHORITY REMARKS	Name and telephone number of shipper preparing this note	17
Hauliers name	Received the above number of packages/containers/trailers in apparent good order and condition unless stated hereon.	BATHUNT (UK) PLC 020 8000 0000	
		Name-/status of declarant A POTTS SHIPPING CLERK	
Vehicle reg. no.		Place and date	
		CROYDON 20/5/03	
Drivers signature	Receiving authority signature and date	Signature of declarant *Potts*	

630 Non-completion of any boxes is a subject for resolution by the contracting parties

3

Documentation required onboard the ship

Dangerous Goods Manifest:

Each ship carrying dangerous goods and marine pollutants shall have on board a special list or manifest setting out the dangerous goods and marine pollutants on board and their locations. Instead of the manifest a detailed stowage plan, which identifies all dangerous goods by class and sets out their location, may be used.

The dangerous goods declaration is used as a basis for making up the manifest and shall at least contain the information from the DG declaration and, *in addition,* should contain the stowage position and the total quantity of the dangerous goods or marine pollutants. A copy of the manifest or stowage plan is made available before departure to the person designated by the port authority.

Emergency Response Information

Appropriate information shall be immediately available for use in emergency response to accidents and incidents involving dangerous goods in transport. The information may be combined with the Dangerous Goods Manifest or stowage plan and must be immediately accessible in the event of an incident.

The manifest or stowage plan may contain references to the emergency schedules found in column 15 of the dangerous goods list. These will be used, in conjunction with the supplement to the IMDG code, to decide on a plan of action for emergencies involving dangerous goods or marine pollutants. In place of the above, separate safety data sheets may be provided for each dangerous cargo or marine pollutant carried.

Document of Compliance

Ships of the following descriptions:

- Passenger ships constructed on or after September 1984

- All other ships of 500 tons or over constructed on or after 1 September 1984;

- All other ships of under 500 tons constructed on or after 1 February 1992

that are intended, or that have cargo spaces intended for, the carriage of dangerous goods on international voyages, must carry a *Document of Compliance.* The document of compliance will certify that the ship complies with regulation 54 of Chapter II-2 to the International Convention for the Safety of Life at Sea 1974 (SOLAS 1974) and will be limited to 5 years from the date of issue.

The document of compliance is issued by the flag state after a survey. This document is usually in the form of a diagram showing all the spaces on board in which dangerous goods can be loaded. A table then sets out the *classes* of dangerous goods that the ship is allowed to carry and the spaces in which these classes can be carried. The document also states additional requirements that must be fulfilled prior to carrying the dangerous goods or marine pollutants. This may be additional fire fighting equipment or ventilation in holds required for certain classes of dangerous goods. [4]

---

[4] *MGN 36 "Document of compliance for ships carrying dangerous goods in solid or dry bulk form", MCA, UK.*

MARINE SAFETY AGENCY

ANNEX

Document of Compliance

Special Requirements for Ships carrying Dangerous Goods

Issued in pursuance of the requirement of regulations II-2/41 & II-2/54.3 of the International Convention for Safety of Life at Sea, 1974, as amended, under the authority of the Government of the United Kingdom of Great Britain and Northern Ireland

Name of ship

Distinctive number or letters   O.N.

Port of registry

Ship type   eg. Ro-Ro Cargo Ferry, Container Ship

IMO Number (if applicable)

THIS IS TO CERTIFY:

1   that the construction and equipment (see note 2) of the above mentioned ship was found to comply with the requirements of regulation II-2/54 of the International Convention for the Safety of Life at Sea, 1974, as amended; and

2.   that the ship is suitable for the carriage of those classes of dangerous goods as specified in the appended schedule 1, subject to any provisions in the International Maritime Dangerous Goods (IMDG) Code and the Code of Safe Practice for Solid Bulk Cargoes (BC Code) for individual substances also being complied with.

This document is valid until the   day of .

Issued at Southampton on the .... of

                                                  ....
                                           (Signature of authorized official issuing the certificate)

NOTE 1:   There are no special requirements in the above-mentioned regulation II-2/54 for the carriage of dangerous goods of classes 6.2 and 7, or for the carriage of dangerous goods in "Limited Quantities", as stated in Section 18 of the General Introduction to the IMDG Code.

NOTE 2:   Schedule 2 lists the special requirements for this ship to carry dangerous goods within the spaces identified in Schedule 1.

Safe Ships Clean Seas

An executive agency of
THE DEPARTMENT OF THE ENVIRONMENT, TRANSPORT AND THE REGIONS

3

118

Schedule 1

The ship is suitable for the carriage of those classes of dangerous goods as specified in the table below, subject to any provisions in the International Maritime Dangerous Goods (IMDG) Code and the Code of Safe Practice for Solid Bulk Cargoes (BC Code) for individual substances also being complied with.

Spaces indicated on the diagram
UNDER-DECK SPACES

ON-DECK SPACES

P = Packaged Goods Permitted

A = Packaged & Bulk Permitted

X = Not Permitted

Class		Space		
	1	2	3	
1.1 - 1.5				
1.4.S				
2.1				
2.2				
2.3				
3.1 + 3.2 (FP < 23°C c.c.)				
3.3 (FP 23°C to 61°C c.c.)				
4.1				
4.2				
4.3				
5.1				
5.2				
6.1 liquids				
6.1 liquids (FP < 23°C c.c.)				
6.1 liquids (FP 23°C to 61°C c.c.)				
6.1 solids				
8 liquids				
8 liquids (FP < 23°C c.c)				
8 liquids (FP 23°C to 61°C c.c)				
8 solids				
9				

NOTE: Cargoes in bulk may be listed individually by name and class

[A number of footnotes may be given here with references to spaces, classes or substances in the table]

4

Extracts from MGN 36 showing spaces and classes of dangerous goods/marine pollutants that can be loaded in those spaces.

Marking and labelling

All packaged dangerous goods must be marked and labelled as per the provisions of the IMDG Code. The marking will include an indication of the hazard class and other details such as the subsidiary risks, elevated temperatures, marine pollutants etc. These markings are required on all four sides of the container and, if the container is bound for an offshore installation, also on the roof.

Marking schemes for Limited Quantities, as per amendment 31, require that the outside of the package be marked with a diamond and with the UN number in the centre (including the letters 'UN' in front of the number). If there is more than one type of dangerous goods in the package the diamond must be large enough to contain the UN numbers for all of them. The package does not have to display the class labels required, the marine pollutant mark, or the shipping name of the material.

All labels must be affixed in a way that they will still be identifiable on packages that have survived at least three months immersion in the sea.

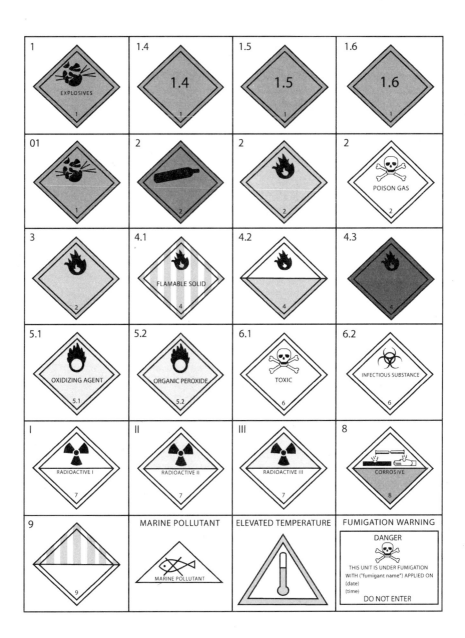

1 EXPLOSIVES 1	**1.4** 1.4 1	**1.5** 1.5 1	**1.6** 1.6 1
01 1	**2** 2	**2** 2	**2** POISON GAS 2
3 2	**4.1** FLAMABLE SOLID 4	**4.2** 4	**4.3** 4
5.1 OXIDIZING AGENT 5.1	**5.2** ORGANIC PEROXIDE 5.2	**6.1** TOXIC 6	**6.2** INFECTIOUS SUBSTANCE 6
I RADIOACTIVE I 7	**II** RADIOACTIVE II 7	**III** RADIOACTIVE III 7	**8** CORROSIVE 8
9 9	**MARINE POLLUTANT** MARINE POLLUTANT	**ELEVATED TEMPERATURE**	**FUMIGATION WARNING** DANGER THIS UNIT IS UNDER FUMIGATION WITH ("fumigant name") APPLIED ON (date) (time) DO NOT ENTER

THE INTERNATIONAL MARITIME DANGEROUS GOODS (IMDG) CODE

KEY POINTS

- The IMDG Code is the primary legal instrument dealing with the stowage, segregation and carriage of dangerous goods by sea.

- The Code applies on domestic or international ferries and cargo ships, operating in rivers, estuary waters or the open sea.

The International Maritime Dangerous Goods (IMDG) Code is an international code for the shipment of dangerous goods by sea. It covers such matters as packing, container traffic and stowage, with emphasis on the segregation of incompatible substances.

IMDG Code

The IMDG Code lays down basic principles for the stowage, segregation and carriage of dangerous substances by sea. It also lays down recommendations for packing, labelling, handling and for emergency response during incidents involving dangerous goods.

Amendments to SOLAS Chapter VII make the IMDG Code mandatory from the 1st of January 2004[1]. The latest amendment to the code is the 32nd amendment, which entered into force on the 1st of January 2005 and is mandatory from the 1st of January 2006.

The major changes to the code, as per amendment 32, are as follows:

- The inclusion of 90 additional UN numbers to cover items such as organo-metallic substances and substances that are toxic by inhalation.

- A new chapter (1.4) regarding Security of Dangerous Goods in transit.

- Many new materials have been added to segregation groups, including the creation of a new category - Alkalis, containing 65 UN numbers. Some acids are now termed "Strong Acids".

- The Class 6.2 and Class 9 sections have been re-written. The transport schedules for Class 7 have been deleted.

- Extensive revisions to Packing Instructions, Construction and Testing of Packaging provisions and a multitude of smaller changes throughout all other chapters.

---

[1] *Amendment 31 to the code makes it mandatory w.e.f 1st January 2004*

<u>Structure of the Code</u>

The two-volume Code is divided into seven parts:

Volume 1 (parts 1, 2 and 4-7 of the Code) contains sections on:

- general provisions, definitions, training
- classification
- packing and tank provisions
- consignment procedures
- construction and testing of packaging, IBCs,large packaging, portable tanks and road tank vehicles
- transport operations

Volume 2 contains:

- The Dangerous Goods List presented in tabular format
- limited quantities exceptions
- the Index
- appendices

The Supplement contains the following texts related to the IMDG Code:

- EMS Guide
- Medical First Aid Guide
- Reporting Procedures
- Packing Cargo Transport Units
- Safe Use of Pesticides
- INF Code

<u>Use of the Code</u>

Prior to loading consignments of dangerous cargo or marine pollutant on board you must refer to the ship specific *Document of Compliance*[2] issued by the flag state or a body authorised by the flag state. This will specify the spaces available on board for loading the dangerous goods and the additional equipment that may be required on board. If the document of compliance allows you to load that

---

[2] *refer to the chapter on "Carriage of dangerous goods" for further information on the document of compliance.*

substance then the next step is to get cargo related information from the cargo specific 'dangerous goods declaration. '

Using the UN number from the dangerous goods declarations, refer to Volume 2 of the Code. The *Dangerous Goods List (DGL)* in Volume 2 of the Code will give additional information about the cargo including its proper shipping name, subsidiary risk and properties.

Stowage

Each substance listed in the dangerous goods list will be allocated a stowage category. Class 1 goods will be allocated a numerical stowage category from 01 to 15, whilst for other classes the stowage requirements are categorised A, B, C, D or E.

The stowage requirements are found in Chapter 7.1 of Volume 1 of the IMDG Code. The stowage requirements range from "on deck stowage only", "on deck or under deck" or "prohibited" depending on the category allocated to the substance and the number of passengers carried by the ship. The Dangerous Goods List (DGL) may also contain additional stowage requirements for individual goods.

Segregation

Once the stowage position has been allocated the next step is to segregate the goods from other substances in the vicinity. The segregation requirements are dealt with in Chapter 7.2 of Volume 1 of the IMDG Code. The segregation requirements between dangerous goods carried on the same ship are laid out in a tabular format. The dangerous goods class of the goods are cross-referenced with the class of the other substance using the following table:

The table gives the segregation requirements as follows:

- *Away from*
- *Separated from*
- *Separated by a complete compartment or hold from*
- *Separated longitudinally by an intervening complete compartment or hold from*

Class	1.1 1.2 1.5	1.3 1.6	1.4	2.1	2.2	2.3	3	4.1	4.2	4.3	5.1	5.2	6.1	6.2	7	8	9
Explosives 1.1, 1.2, 1.5	*	*	*	4	2	2	4	4	4	4	4	4	2	4	2	4	x
Explosives 1.3, 1.6	*	*	*	4	2	2	4	3	3	4	4	4	2	4	2	2	x
Explosives 1.4	*	*	*	2	1	1	2	2	2	2	2	2	x	4	2	2	x
Flammable gasses 2.1	4	4	2	x	x	x	2	1	2	x	2	2	x	4	2	1	x
Non-toxic, non-flammable gases 2.2	2	2	1	x	x	x	1	x	1	x	x	1	x	2	1	x	x
Toxic gasses 2.3	2	2	1	x	x	x	2	x	2	x	x	2	x	2	1	x	x
Flammable liquids 3	4	4	2	2	1	2	x	x	2	1	2	2	x	3	2	x	x
Flammable solids**) 4.1	4	3	2	1	x	x	x	x	1	x	1	2	x	3	2	1	x
Substances liable to spontaneous combustion 4.2	4	3	2	2	1	2	2	1	x	1	2	2	1	3	2	1	x
Substances which, in contact with water, emit flammable gasses 4.3	4	4	2	x	x	x	1	x	1	x	2	2	x	2	2	1	x
Oxidizing substances (agents) 5.1	4	4	2	2	x	x	2	1	2	2	x	2	1	3	1	2	x
Organic peroxides 5.2	4	4	2	2	1	2	2	2	2	2	2	x	1	3	2	2	x
Toxic substances 6.1	2	2	x	x	x	x	x	x	1	x	1	1	x	1	x	x	x
Infectious substances 6.2	4	4	4	4	2	2	3	3	3	2	3	3	1	x	3	3	x
Radioactive materials 7	2	2	2	2	1	1	2	2	2	2	1	2	x	3	x	2	x
Corrosives 8	4	2	2	1	x	x	x	1	1	1	2	2	x	3	2	x	x
Miscellaneous dangerous substances and articles 9	x	x	x	x	x	x	x	x	x	x	x	x	x	x	x	x	x

If the segregation requirements are given as an "X" then the requirements, if any, between the two substances will be found in the "properties and observations" column in the dangerous goods list (IMDG Volume 2).

Segregation between substances of Class 1 is found in the introduction to Class 1 chapter in Volume 1 of the code.

The next step is to refer these segregation requirements to the ship specific tables. There are separate tables for the following:

- Segregation of packages

- Segregation of freight containers on board container ships

- Segregation of cargo transport units aboard ro-ro ships

- Segregation between bulk materials possessing chemical hazards and dangerous goods in packaged form

For example, referring to the table that follows, for a ro-ro vessel, the segregation requirement "*away from*" will mean the following:

Closed cargo transport units: no restrictions for their stowage in either the fore and aft direction or the athwartships direction.

Open transport units: a distance of at least three metres must be maintained between the units.

Table of segregation of cargo transport units on board ro-ro ships

SEGREGATION REQUIREMENT		HORIZONTAL					
		CLOSED VERSUS CLOSED		CLOSED VERSUS OPEN		OPEN VERSUS OPEN	
		ON DECK	UNDER DECK	ON DECK	UNDER DECK	ON DECK	UNDER DECK
"AWAY FROM" .1	FORE AND AFT	NO RESTRICTION	NO RESTRICTION	NO RESTRICTION	NO RESTRICTION	AT LEAST 3 METRES	AT LEAST 3 METRES
	ATHWART-SHIPS	NO RESTRICTION	NO RESTRICTION	NO RESTRICTION	NO RESTRICTION	AT LEAST 3 METRES	AT LEAST 3 METRES
"SEPERATED FROM" .2	FORE AND AFT	AT LEAST 6 METRES	AT LEAST 6 METRES OR ONE BULKHEAD	AT LEAST 6 METRES	AT LEAST 6 METRES OR ONE BULKHEAD	AT LEAST 6 METRES	AT LEAST 12 METRES OR ONE BULKHEAD
	ATHWART-SHIPS	AT LEAST 3 METRES	AT LEAST 3 METRES OR ONE BULKHEAD	AT LEAST 3 METRES	AT LEAST 6 METRES OR ONE BULKHEAD	AT LEAST 6 METRES	AT LEAST 12 METRES OR ONE BULKHEAD
"SEPERATED BY A COMPLETE COMPARTMENT OR HOLD FROM" .3	FORE AND AFT	AT LEAST 12 METRES	AT LEAST 24 METRES + DECK	AT LEAST 24 METRES	AT LEAST 24 METRES + DECK	AT LEAST 36 METRES	TWO DECKS OR TWO BULKHEADS
	ATHWART-SHIPS	AT LEAST 12 METRES	AT LEAST 24 METRES + DECK	AT LEAST 24 METRES	AT LEAST 24 METRES + DECK	PROHIBITED	PROHIBITED
"SEPERATED LONGITUDINALLY BY AN INTERVENING COMPLETE COMPARTMENT OR HOLD FROM" .4	FORE AND AFT	AT LEAST 36 METRES	TWO BULKHEADS OR AT LEAST 36 METRES + TWO DECKS	AT LEAST 36 METRES	AT LEAST 48 METRES INCLUDING TWO BULKHEADS	AT LEAST 48 METRES	PROHIBITED
	ATHWART-SHIPS	PROHIBITED	PROHIBITED	PROHIBITED	PROHIBITED	PROHIBITED	PROHIBITED

NOTE: ALL BULKHEADS AND DECKS SHOULD BE RESISTANT TO FIRE AND LIQUID

Emergencies involving dangerous goods:

The supplement to the IMDG Code contains the emergency schedules for fire and spillage involving dangerous goods. Medical emergencies are covered in the Medical First Aid Guide (MFAG), and also in the supplement to the Code.

The Dangerous Goods List (Column 15) in Volume 2 contains references to the emergency schedules for spillage or fire for individual UN numbers. The first code is the fire schedule and the second code the spillage schedule.

Fire Schedules

There are 10 fire schedules, including a General Fire Schedule (F-A) and nine further schedules (F-B to F-J) dealing with particular groups of hazardous goods. Each schedule starts with a list of the UN numbers to which the schedule may be applicable. The schedule then starts with general comments on the danger of the cargo followed by sections dealing with cargoes on fire on deck, cargoes on fire under deck and cargoes exposed to fire. Most fire schedules then have a section dealing with special cases related to particular UN numbered cargoes. The notes on specific chemicals are generally more detailed than those in the last version.

Spillage Schedule

The 26 spillage schedules start with S-A, toxic substances, and end with S-Z, toxic explosives. As with the fire schedules, each starts with the list of applicable UN numbers. The sections generally correspond to the fire schedule ones but there is more differentiation between large and small spillages.

Medical First Aid Guide (MFAG)

In case of an emergency involving dangerous goods, the MFAG in the supplement to the IMDG Code should be referred to. This is arranged into three sections:

- A flowchart based emergency action and diagnosis
- Tables giving brief instructions for special circumstances
- Appendices giving comprehensive information, a list of medicines/drugs, and a list of chemicals referred to in the table.

The supplement to the IMDG Code also contains the following:

- Reporting procedures for accidents and incidents involving dangerous goods
- Guidelines for Packing Cargo Transport Units
- International Code for the Safe Carriage of Packaged Irradiated Nuclear Fuel (INF Code)
- Recommendations for the Safe Use of Pesticides at Sea

SECTION TWO: LIQUID AND GAS CARGOES

PETROLEUM CARGOES – HAZARDS

KEY POINTS

- All personnel involved in the carriage of petroleum cargoes must be familiar with the hazards inherent in them

- Knowledge of these hazards and the methods to reduce or eliminate them is critical for the safe transportation of petroleum product cargoes

The main hazards that are inherent in petroleum cargoes are:

- Flammability
- Toxicity
- Pollution

Flammability

This is the primary hazard to be aware of during the carriage of petroleum cargoes. Petroleum vapour is easily ignited and burns with a visible flame. The level of flammability of a liquid is determined by its *volatility* and temperature, as these two factors determine the amount of vapour that will be released. It is always the vapour that ignites and burns and not the liquid itself.

This vapour forms the fuel side of the fire triangle depicted below.

Petroleum cargoes are generally divided into two broad categories that are based on their volatility and their *Flashpoint[1]*

- *Non-Volatile* Liquids are those with a flashpoint of 60 degrees Celsius or above, as determined by the closed cup method of testing.

- *Volatile* Liquids are those with a flashpoint below 60 degrees Celsius, as determined by the closed cup method.

---

[1] *Flashpoint is defined as the lowest temperature at which sufficient gases are evolved at the surface of the liquid to ignite when a naked flame is passed over it.*

The vapour given out by petroleum cargoes can only burn if it is mixed with air in certain proportions. If there is too much or too little vapour in the air mixture the vapour will not burn. These limiting proportions, expressed as a percentage by volume of petroleum gas in air, are known as the lower and the upper flammable limits.

The *Lower Flammable Limit (LFL)* is that hydrocarbon concentration below which there is insufficient hydrocarbon gas to support and propagate combustion. The mixture is said to be *too lean.*

The *Upper Flammable Limit (UFL)* is that hydrocarbon concentration above which there is insufficient air to support combustion. The mixture in this case is said to be *too rich.*

For normal petroleum cargoes the lower and upper flammable limits are usually between 1% and 10% by volume.

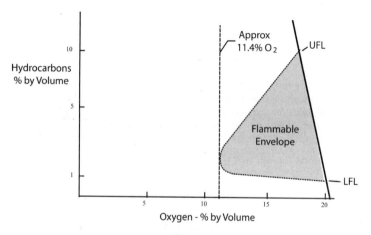

Oxygen - % by Volume

This *Flammable Range Diagram* depicts the flammable limits and the *Flammable Envelope* is the range in which combustion can occur. To prevent ignition it must be ensured that the atmosphere in the tank never passes through the flammable envelope

Sources of ignition

The main sources of ignition on board a tanker are:

- Direct Heat - smoking, naked flames etc.
  Restricting the smoking areas on board a tanker to certain designated areas can stop this.
  All equipment used on deck must be intrinsically safe and certified for use in a flammable atmosphere.
  No naked flames must be allowed on deck and the carriage of lighters and matchboxes must be forbidden.

- Mechanical Sparks – Chipping, dropped tools etc.
  Opinion is divided as to whether sparks caused due to chipping etc. can

cause ignition, but as far as possible these activities must be restricted onboard a tanker. A risk assessment and permit to work system must be in use on board. A tool belt must be worn if entering tanks to prevent sparks from falling metal tools

- Electrical Sparks – Lightning, static discharge, electric arcing etc.
  All electrical equipment in use on decks and in gas dangerous areas must be intrinsically safe.
  All cargo and venting operations must be suspended if lightning is spotted in the vicinity.
  Unauthorised use of cameras, radios, mobile phones,Mp3 players, etc. must be forbidden.

- Chemical Energy – Spontaneous combustion, auto–ignition, pyrophoric iron sulphide, Metallic Smears etc.
  Spontaneous combustion can occur in the case of certain substances. For example oily rags left in the open are at risk of igniting. Spontaneous combustion is the ignition of a material brought about by a heat producing chemical reaction within the material itself, without exposure to an external source of ignition.
  Static electricity is the electricity produced when dissimilar materials with opposing charges are brought close together. Certain oils are capable of retaining a static charge and these are known as static accumulator oils. Particular care must be taken prior to introducing an unearthed object (for measuring ullage etc) into a tank containing static accumulator oils. The ullage tape must always be earthed to dissipate the charge prior to introducing it into the tank.

The flow of oil in pipelines and the dropping of oil on the tank top when loading may also cause static charges. The amount of water in the tank or in the oil also influences the static charge. Spraying water into the tanks during water washing can also give rise to an electrically charged mist. For this reason initial loading rates must be slow and excess moisture must be prevented from entering the tank. To reduce the static generation properties of static accumulator oils the shipper may add an anti-static additive.

Pyrophoric Iron Sulphide is iron sulphide capable of a rapid exothermic oxidation causing incandescence and the ignition of any hydrocarbon–air mixtures when exposed to air. When any rust in the tank comes in contact with hydrogen sulphide, iron sulphide is formed. This reverts back to iron oxide in the presence of air and gives off heat and light. To prevent this, tanks must be kept inerted and rust free.

Metallic smears are caused when two dissimilar metals (e.g. aluminium and steel) are rubbed together, resulting in a metal deposit being formed. This can cause a chemical reaction, which gives off heat, between the metals.

LIVERPOOL JOHN MOORES UNIVERSITY
LEARNING & INFORMATION SERVICES

Toxicity

Petroleum liquids and the vapour produced are inherently toxic and harmful to the personnel exposed to them. A number of indicators are used to measure the concentrations of toxic vapours and the main unit of measurement is the *Threshold Limit Value (TLV)*.

TLV is defined as the average concentration of a substance to which workers may be exposed for a set time period. The values are expressed as parts per million (ppm) by volume of gas in air. It is more closely defined as follows:

TLV-TWA (Time Weighted Average)- this is the average concentration of a substance to which workers may be repeatedly exposed, for a normal 8-hour workday or a 40-hour week, day after day, without adverse effects. Any reference to TLV on safety data sheets is usually the TLV-TWA.

TLV-STEL (Short Term Exposure Limit) this is the maximum concentration of a substance to which workers may be exposed for a maximum period of 15 minutes. Four such exposures are allowed during a working day with an interval of at least one hour between each.

TLV-C (Ceiling) this is the upper limit above which workers should never be exposed to the substance.

The main ways that exposure can occur are as follows:

- Ingestion
  Generally the risk of swallowing significant quantities of liquid petroleum during normal operational practice is slight. If petroleum is swallowed is causes acute discomfort and nausea. There is a possibility that liquid petroleum can be drawn into the lungs during vomiting and this can have serious consequences.

- Skin Contact
  Petroleum products can cause skin irritation and may lead to dermatitis. They are also very irritating to the eyes and prolonged exposure can have serious effects. Direct contact with petroleum products must be avoided and proper PPE must be worn.

- Inhalation
  The main effect of petroleum gas inhalation on personnel is to produce narcosis. The symptoms range from eye irritation to headache and a feeling of light-headedness at higher concentrations. At very high concentrations inhalation can lead to paralysis, insensibility or even death.
  The toxicity of petroleum products depends on individual constituents. Toxicity can be greatly influenced by the presence of constituents like benzene and hydrogen sulphide. The smell of petroleum gases cannot be depended upon as an indicator of increasing concentrations, as in some cases the sense of smell may be dulled, especially if the mixture contains Hydrogen Sulphide. The absence of smell should never be taken to indicate the absence of vapour.

Ref: ISGOTT

PIPELINE SYSTEMS

KEY POINTS

- Different types of pipeline systems exist for cargo operations on crude and product tankers

- The advantages and disadvantages of each type must be known in order to carry out safe loading and discharging operations

There are four basic types of pipeline systems in existence, namely:

- Ring Main
- Direct Line
- Free Flow
- Cruciform

Pipeline systems on individual tankers may consist of a mixture of one or more of the above types and will differ from other ships in terms of the positioning of the pumps and valves.

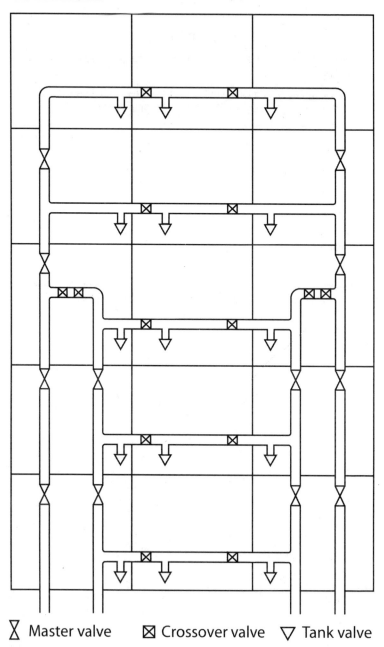

X Master valve   ⊠ Crossover valve   ▽ Tank valve

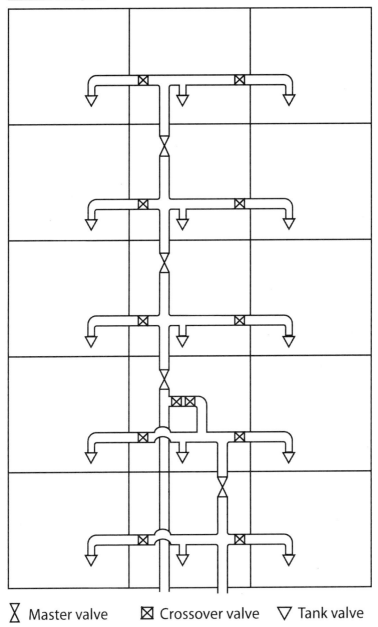

X Master valve   ⊠ Crossover valve   ▽ Tank valve

Ring Main

This is found only on older types of product tankers.

Advantages

- Versatile – any pump can be configured to discharge any tank
- Good Segregation – a high degree of tank separation is possible

Disadvantages

- Expensive – both in construction and maintenance due to the large number of bends and joints required
- Poor Flow Rate – due to the restriction imposed by the bends.

Direct Line

This pipeline system is generally found in VLCC's.

Advantages

- Fast loading and discharge rates due to fewer bends
- Cheap to construct
- Low maintenance costs
- Line washing time reduced

Disadvantages

- Not very versatile and cannot handle two or more grades.
- Small number of valves can lead to poor segregation and less possibility of containing leaks

Free Flow System Diagram

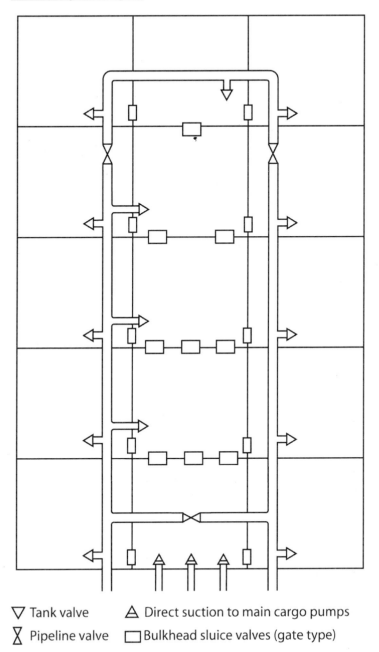

▽ Tank valve   △ Direct suction to main cargo pumps

⊗ Pipeline valve   ☐ Bulkhead sluice valves (gate type)

Cruciform System Diagram

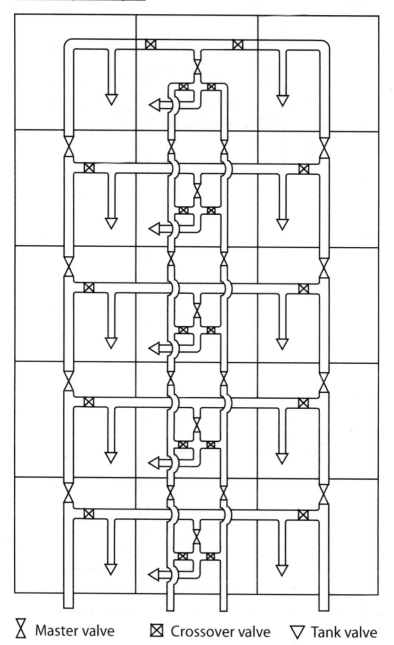

⎇ Master valve ⊠ Crossover valve ▽ Tank valve

Free Flow System

This system, which allows for very fast discharge and turnaround times, was generally fitted to large crude oil tankers like VLCC's and ULCC's in the early 1970s, though it is rarely seen now because of its disadvantage of grade separation

Advantages

- Fast loading and discharging. There are sluice valves fitted in tank adjoining bulkheads, and these allow for very fast flow towards the pump room when the ship is trimmed by the stern.

- Efficient line and tank drainage

Disadvantages

- Carriage of more than one grade virtually impossible

Cruciform System

This type of system combines the advantages of the ring main and the direct line systems and is now found on the majority of modern product carriers.

Advantages

- Very versatile allowing two or more grades to be simultaneously loaded and discharged

- Good segregation between grades

- Possibility of interchanging system using spool pieces

Disadvantages

- Expensive to install

- The large number of bends makes line cleaning difficult

INERT GAS SYSTEMS

KEY POINTS

- Inert Gas systems are a key component of the cargo handling process on tankers

- SOLAS Chapter II-2 regulates the technical and operational requirements for IG systems

---

Inert Gas is defined as a gas or a mixture of gases, such as flue gas, that contain insufficient oxygen to support the combustion of hydrocarbons. The main purpose of inert gas, in terms of cargo operations on tankers, is to prevent the formation of a flammable atmosphere in the cargo tanks. As can be seen in the chapter on *Hazards of Petroleum Cargoes*, the three components required for ignition are fuel, heat and oxygen. In atmospheres where the oxygen content is below 11.5% by volume, ignition is not possible. On a tanker the cargo vapour is always present, which provides the fuel side of the fire triangle. Even though sources of ignition can be restricted, they can never be eliminated. So, the best way to prevent combustion is to use inert gas and restrict oxygen. With an inert gas system the protection against a tank explosion is achieved by introducing inert gas into the tank to keep the oxygen content low and so reduce to safe proportions the hydrocarbon gas concentration of the tank atmosphere.

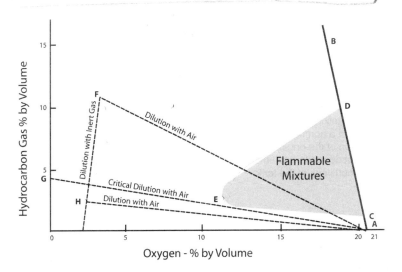

As seen from the diagram above, when an inert gas is added to a hydrocarbon gas/air mixture (point F on the diagram) the result is a reduction in the concentration of hydrocarbons in the mixture to below the lower flammable limit (LFL) – point H on the diagram. At this point air can safely be introduced into the tank as the concentration of hydrocarbons in the atmosphere will always be below the LFL until, finally, there is 21% oxygen in the tank – point A on the diagram. The other alternative, diluting with air from point F will cause the mixture to be within the flammable range - along line FA in the diagram. Line AG is the *Critical Dilution Line* that divides the safe area below the LFL from the unsafe area immediately above.

Sources

The possible sources of inert gas on board a tanker are:

- The uptake from the main or auxiliary boilers
- An independent IG generator
- A gas turbine plant, when equipped with an after burner

All the above sources should be able to deliver inert gas (IG) to the tanks with a maximum oxygen content of less than 5% by volume.

Gas Replacement Processes

Replacement of gas in cargo tanks is needed for the following reasons:

- Inerting, to replace the air with inert gas
- Purging, to replace inert gas with cargo vapours
- Gas freeing, to replace inert gas with air

These operations can be carried out using one of two processes of gas replacement, which are:

- Dilution
- Displacement.

Dilution is a mixing process whereby the incoming gas mixes with the original gases to form a homogenous mixture throughout the tank. As a result the concentration of the original gas decreases exponentially. The actual rate of gas replacement depends upon the volume flow of the incoming gas, its entry velocity and the dimensions of the tank.

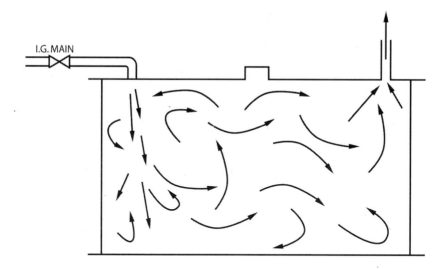

I.G. MAIN

Displacement relies on a stable horizontal interface between the incoming gas and the replaced gas. Usually, the heavier inert gas is introduced from the bottom while the lighter air is vented from the top. As inert gas is introduced via the loading line, i.e. from the bottom of the tank, air is vented from the top of the tank. It is critical when using the displacement method, to continually monitor the tank atmosphere and adjust flow rates to prevent mixing of the gases.

In practice the best way to change atmospheres depends on the individual ships' cargo operating manual, recommendations, pipeline systems, IG equipment and practical experience

Inert Gas System Requirements

As per SOLAS Chapter II-2, regulation 60, an inert gas system is required for the following ship types:

- All tankers of 20,000 DWT and upwards;
- All tankers engaged in crude oil washing (COW)

The inert gas and associated venting system must allow for the following operations to be conducted safely (*regulation 62 of SOLAS chapter II-2*):

- Gas Freeing
- Purging
- Inerting
- Expansion and contraction of oil in the cargo tank
- Cargo and Ballast handling
- Tank Entry
- Must be capable of *supplying* Inert Gas to all cargo tanks at a rate greater than the maximum discharge rate of the Cargo (125%).
- Must be capable of supplying Inert Gas with oxygen content less than 5% by volume *in the inert gas supply main* to the cargo tanks at any given rate of flow.

The following are the systems approved by SOLAS for IG systems:

- Treated flue gas systems from main or auxiliary boilers.
- Inert gas generators.
- CO_2, but only where approved by the administration

For double hull tankers the double hull spaces must be fitted with suitable connections for the supply of air and, on ships fitted with an IG system, suitable connections for the supply of IG.

Inert Gas System Layout

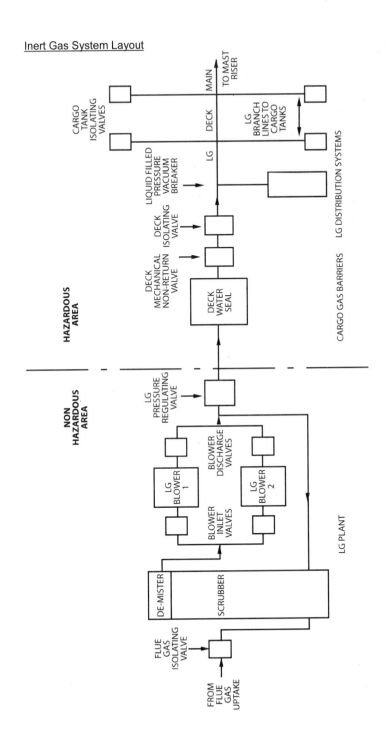

A typical inert gas system on a crude oil tanker consists of the following components:

- Source i.e. flue gas
- Scrubbing tower
- Fans/blowers
- Oxygen monitors
- Deck water seal
- Mechanical non return valves
- Pressure/Vacuum breaker
- Branch line to tank
- Pressure/Vacuum valve
- Mast Riser

Scrubbing Tower

Flue gas cannot be directly introduced into the cargo tanks as it is at a temperature of about 300 degrees Celsius and contains a variety of impurities, including soot and Sulphur Dioxide. The function of the scrubbing tower is to cool and clean the flue gas, using sea water, to remove the solid particles and reduce the Sulphur Dioxide content.

After leaving the Boiler Uptake the gas enters the base of the Scrubber. After passing through the pre-cooling water spray the hot gas enters the base of the Scrubber via a water seal. The hot gas then flows upwards through a zone of high capacity sprays and various impingement baffle plate stages.

The gas finally exits at the top of the scrubber cooled to within 2 degrees of the sea water temperature and with 99% of soluble particles and Sulphur Dioxide removed. The gas then passes through demisters to remove any water entrained in the gas stream. The water extracted is drained overboard via a drain valve.

The following alarms are fitted:

- High water level
- Low water level

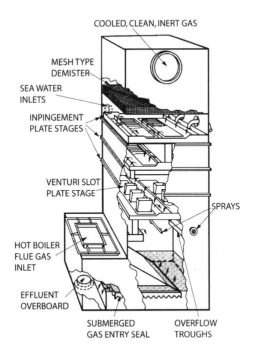

COOLED, CLEAN, INERT GAS

MESH TYPE DEMISTER

SEA WATER INLETS

INPINGEMENT PLATE STAGES

VENTURI SLOT PLATE STAGE

SPRAYS

HOT BOILER FLUE GAS INLET

EFFLUENT OVERBOARD

SUBMERGED GAS ENTRY SEAL

OVERFLOW TROUGHS

Fans

These are usually two high capacity blowers. They can be electric or turbine driven centrifugal fans. The fan has carbon gland seals to ensure gas tightness. The combined capacity of the fans must be at least 125% of the maximum discharge rate to satisfy SOLAS requirements. There is a fresh air intake valve before the blowers. This can be used to aerate the tanks after inerting once the IG system has been shut down.

Fixed Oxygen Analysers

Fixed oxygen monitors are fitted on the discharge side of the blowers. They have to be calibrated before use and they alarm if the oxygen content exceeds the SOLAS maximum of 5% by volume.

Deck Water Seal

The purpose of the Deck Water Seal is to prevent the backflow of hydrocarbon gases from the cargo tanks to the Engine Room and Boiler Uptakes via the Inert Gas Main. A mechanical non return valve may permit a small amount of hydrocarbon gas to pass through. To prevent this, the Deck Water Seal is used, which is a non mechanical non return valve.

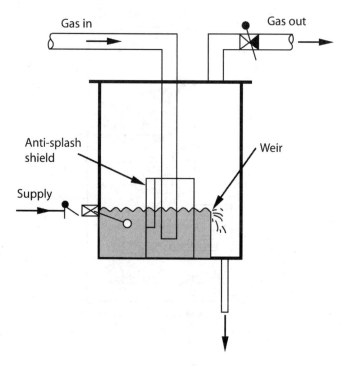

The basic form of Deck Water Seal is the wet type, in which the gas passes through a water reservoir and a demister before exiting to the deck main. As long as the gas pressure is more than the pressure in the tanks there is no danger of a backflow. In case the inert gas pressure falls, creating a danger of a backflow, the water forms a plug and hydrostatic head, preventing the flow of hydrocarbon gasses back to the boiler uptakes.

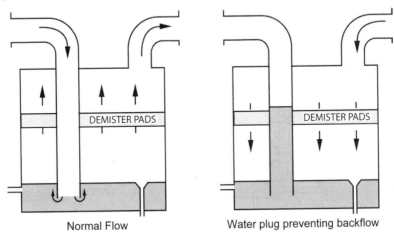

Normal Flow   Water plug preventing backflow

The disadvantage of a "wet" type seal is that water carry-over may be high, resulting in increased corrosion. Hence a dry type or a semi-dry type may be used.

Dry Type Seal

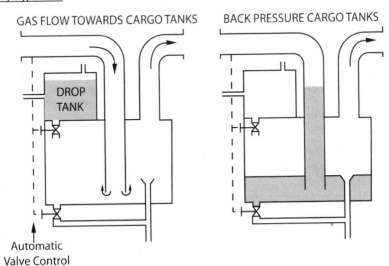

GAS FLOW TOWARDS CARGO TANKS   BACK PRESSURE CARGO TANKS

Automatic
Valve Control

In a dry type seal, a sensor releases water from a holding tank if a loss of pressure is detected. The advantage is that there is no water carry over, but there is a risk of failure of the automatic control valves rendering the system ineffective.

Semi-dry type

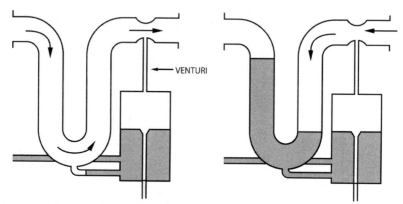

VENTURI

In a semi-dry type of deck water seal the inert gas flow passing a venturi draws the sealing water into a separate holding chamber by vacuum action, thus reducing the water carry-over. The disadvantage of this system is that a blockage of the venturi tubes may allow water into the U bend. Alternatively a blockage of the tube leading to the U bend may prevent water from entering the seal and render the system ineffective.

Mechanical Non Return Valves

After the Deck Water Seal, and as a further precaution to prevent the backflow of gases from the cargo tanks, as well as to prevent any backflow of liquid that may enter the inert gas main if the cargo tanks are overfilled, a mechanical non-return valve is fitted. This should operate automatically at all times, and is generally in the form of a one-way flap. This valve may commonly be referred to as the 'donking' valve.

A separate deck isolating valve may be fitted forward of the non-return valve, so that the inert gas main can be isolated from the non-return valve for maintenance on the system.

Pressure/Vacuum Breaker

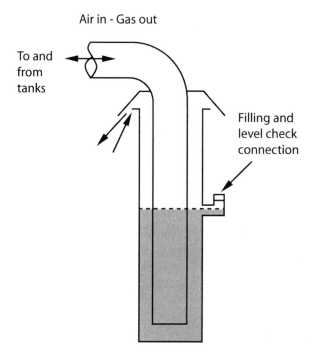

Air in - Gas out

To and from tanks

Filling and level check connection

A Pressure Vacuum Breaker is fitted on the inert gas line to guard against over pressurisation or creation of vacuum in the system.

The Pressure Vacuum Breaker consists of an outer chamber that is mounted on a base on the Main Deck. The outer chamber is filled with a water-glycol mixture to prevent freezing in the winter. In case of over pressurisation the liquid in the outer chamber is displaced relieving the IG line pressure. In case of under pressurisation, the liquid is drawn into the line, this breaking the vacuum.

Pressure Vacuum Valves

In addition to the P/V breaker, to prevent over pressurisation or under pressurisation and to allow for the normal expansion and contraction of oil, Pressure Vacuum Valves (P/V valves) are fitted on individual tanks or on individual mast risers connected to tanks.

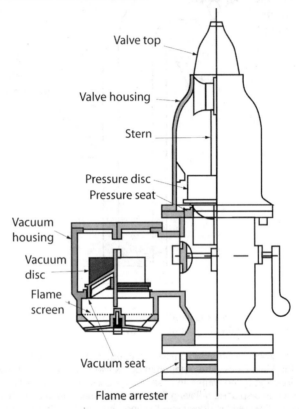

The P/V valves are set to operate between about 2100mm water gauge (WG) pressure & 350mm WG vacuum. In case of an increase in pressure the pressure disc lifts venting IG and in case of under pressurisation, the vacuum disc lifts allowing outside air to break the vacuum.

According to SOLAS regulation 59, to prevent over pressurisation, secondary P/V relief system is to be provided to back-up the primary P/V Valves. Alternatively, tank pressure sensors can be installed with alarms for over or under pressure condition.

While this valve is generally regarded as a back-up to the primary system, it is also an independent fail safe system to protect the tank should it be isolated from the Inert Gas main

<u>Mast Risers</u>

Mast Risers are fitted to vent off inert gas or air to the atmosphere. Modern tankers are fitted with vapour recovery and vapour return systems. Mast risers are fitted with spark arresters as safety features. There is also an isolation valve at the base and, if the mast riser is for an individual tank, a pressure vacuum valve may be fitted.

<u>Safety Features and Alarms for Inert Gas Systems</u>

- Low water pressure/flow to the scrubber
- High water level in scrubber
- High I.G. temperature

Any of these alarms should cause automatic shut down of the blowers and regulating valves.

Other alarms required by SOLAS are:

- Failure of I.G. blowers, (the gas regulating valve should close).
- O2 content > 5% by volume.
- Failure of power supply to the regulating valve control system.
- Low water level in the Deck Water Seal
- Low I.G pressure < 100mm W.G.
- High I.G. pressure.

Additional requirements for I.G. generators:

- Insufficient fuel supply
- Power failure to the generator
- Power failure to the control system

References:

Inert Gas Systems, 1990 edition, IMO London.
Petroleum Tankship Cargo Handling Manual; Lorne & Maclean; Polytech International, 1979.

CRUDE OIL WASHING

KEY POINTS

- Crude oil washing has many advantages over water washing and reduces operational pollution

- A crude oil tanker with an inert gas system and approved fixed washing equipment can use crude oil as a washing medium

---

Crude oil washing (COW) is the name given to the method of cleaning out the tanks on a crude oil tanker, by means of high-pressure jet nozzles, with the crude oil cargo itself ("oil to remove oil") at pressures of 9-10 kg/cm2. This operation can take place either in port or at sea between discharge ports.

Crude Oil Washing

The solvent action of the crude oil makes the cleaning process far more effective than when water only is being used. A subsequent water wash would be conducted prior to gas freeing the tank for entry or introduction of clean ballast. This system helps to prevent pollution of the seas from operational measures and maximises cargo outturn.

The requirement for new crude oil tankers to be built with double hulls, has further improved the efficiency of COW operations because more of the structural support members are placed outside the cargo tanks, greatly reducing the amount of crude oil residues left in the tank following discharge.

MARPOL requirements

MARPOL Annex I Regulation 13 (6) requires every new crude oil tanker of 20,000 tons Dwt and above to be fitted crude oil washing systems.

On 'pre-MARPOL' tankers, i.e. those without Segregated Ballast Tanks[1], the cargo tanks designated for dirty ballast[2] and clean ballast[3] must have been crude oil washed prior to the introduction of ballast water.

---

[1] Segregated Ballast Tanks (SBT) are ballast tanks with their own closed system that is segregated from the cargo oil system. These tanks are ballast tanks that only contain ballast water
[2] Dirty Ballast – This is the term for ballast water that has been loaded in to a cargo tank that previously contained oil, but the tank has been crude oil washed
[3] Clean Ballast – This is the term for ballast water that has been loaded in to a cargo tank that previously contained oil, but the tank has been crude oil washed and subsequently water washed

On ships with segregated ballast tanks, approximately 25% of the crude oil tanks need to be washed on every voyage for sludge control purposes such that no tank needs to be washed more than once in every four months.

For tankers with insufficient SBT capacity, an appropriate number of cargo tanks will need to be crude oil washed, such that when subsequently water washed these tanks will be "clean" enough (as defined by MARPOL) to take on sufficient water ballast to achieve the required draught on voyage.

The COW installation and arrangements onboard a tanker should comply with the provisions of the *"Specifications for the Design, Operation and Control of Crude Oil Washing Systems"* adopted by the International Maritime Organization (IMO) in 1978.

In addition to these regulatory requirements, charter parties and commercial contracts may require the ship owner to carry out crude oil washing to a greater extent than legislation dictates in order to maximize the cargo outturn.

Operational Procedures

When it is necessary to carry out crude oil washing during cargo discharge, the Master must inform the terminal at least 24 hours in advance of the operation. Crude oil washing should only be carried out when approval is received from the terminal.

Only fixed tank washing machines can be used to carry out crude oil washing. Prior to the operation, a safety checklist is completed. An inert gas system must be in operation and the oxygen content of the tank atmosphere must not exceed either 8% by volume or the minimum level required by the terminal. Personnel in charge of the operation must be qualified and must have completed an approved training course, either on board or in a training institution.

Before arrival in port the following must be carried out:

- Tank washing system pressure tested to normal working pressure and examined for leaks before arriving in port

- All machines should be operated and any leaks found should be made good.

During crude oil washing the system must be kept under constant observation so that any leak can be detected and the necessary action taken.

Mixtures of oil and water can create an electrically charged mist during washing. Therefore only "dry"[4] crude should be used for crude oil washing and any tank that is to be used as a source for COW must be partly discharged (at least one metre) prior to operation. If the slop tank is to be used, it should first be completely discharged ashore and refilled with "dry" crude oil.

---

[4] Dry Crude - Dry crude: Crude with minimum water content. In practice, before crude oil washing, tank soundings are reduced by about a meter (debottoming); this removes the free water which will settle below the crude oil in the tank. This is done to reduce the danger of static electricity when crude oil washing.

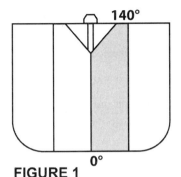

FIGURE 1
Full wash nozzle.
Set to operate between
0° and 140°

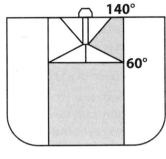

FIGURE 2
Washing during discharge.
Tank one-third discharged
nozzle set to operate
continuously between
60° and 140°

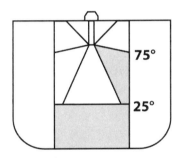

FIGURE 3
Tank two-thirds discharged.
Nozzle set to operate
continuously between
25° and 75°

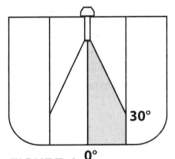

FIGURE 4
Bottom washing.
Nozzle set to operate
continuously between
0° and 25°

Crude oil washing can cause excess hydrocarbon emissions. Subsequent ballasting of the tanks can cause this gas to be expelled to the atmosphere. Terminals may not allow this, so the following are among the means used to reduce vapour emission:

- Permanent ballast tanks of sufficient capacity
- Retention of the gas in the cargo tank system by simultaneous ballasting and cargo discharge

- Gas compression method
- On completion of the discharge, the tank pressure is at a minimum and all cargo tanks are common via the inert gas line.
- Gases from the ballasted cargo tanks are transferred through the inert gas lines into the available cargo tank space.
- A suitable combination of any of these vapour methods.

Advantages of crude oil washing

- Increased cargo outturn as clingage and deposits are reduced.
- Reduction in the time for pre-dock cleaning
- Reduces operational pollution
- Minimum manual desludging required
- Reduction in ballast passage tank cleaning
- Less sea water discharged to shore
- Less tank corrosion

Disadvantages of crude oil washing

- Increased work load in port
- Increase in discharge time
- Increased vapour emissions
- Additional training for crew required
- Additional pipe work, hence more possibilities of leaks
- Higher capital costs for installation

Possible "COW" abort situations

- Inert gas plant failure
- High oxygen content in tank
- Failure of the oxygen detectors
- Leakage in joint or pipeline
- Tank overflow
- Emergency alarms
- Failure of the tank gauging system
- Poor weather conditions
- Failure of communications
- Changes in ullage for tanks that are not being discharged
- Hydrocarbon emissions in excess of terminal requirements

OIL & PRODUCT TANKERS - OPERATIONS

KEY POINTS

- Loading, discharging and cargo care on an oil or product tanker is a potentially hazardous operation

- Procedures must be put in place and followed to ensure a safe operation

---

Before any cargo operations are carried out the master of the ship and the terminal operator must:

- Agree in writing the handling procedures, including the maximum loading and discharge rates

- Complete and sign the Ship/Shore safety checklist, which shows the main safety precautions to be taken before and during the cargo transfer operation

- Agree in writing the actions that are to be taken in the case of an emergency during the cargo transfer operation.

Completion of the Ship/Shore Safety Checklist ensures that the terminal and the ship have made the necessary preparations for the safe transfer of the cargo. Some of the checklist questions are directed at the terminal, some questions are for the ship and others apply to both ship and terminal. The checklist must not be signed until both parties are satisfied that the standards of safety on both sides are fully acceptable. Part "A" of the checklist deals with bulk liquid general, which applies to all tankers. Part "B" and "C" apply to chemical and gas tankers respectively.

Loading

After completion of the Ship/Shore safety checklist the cargo transfer operations can commence. Prior to loading, the stability of the ship will be calculated and checked. As deballasting will be carried out concurrently with the loading operations, it must be ensured that there are no excessive free surface effects that could lead to a loss of stability. This is especially important for double hull tankers as the "U" shaped ballast tanks can give rise to significant free surface effects when the water level falls below the wing tank level. Ballast and loading operations must be carried out in a way such that the ship's hull is never subject to excessive stresses.

Inert Gas Procedures

During loading the inert gas plant must be closed down. Inert gas pressures in the tanks to be loaded must be reduced prior to the commencement of loading.

During loading the following sequence of operations are carried out:

- Agree on maximum loading rates with the terminal
- Ensure that the Ship/Shore Safety Checklist is completed
- Ensure that an emergency shutdown procedure is agreed between the ship and the shore
- Line-up according to the loading plan and double check the position of the valves.
- For closed loading ensure that the ullage, sounding and sighting ports are closed.
- The inert gas displaced by the loading operation is usually vented to the atmosphere via the mast riser or, if the terminal is so equipped, the vapours can be returned ashore using a vapour return line
- When line up is done and verified the terminal must be informed and the manifold valves opened.
- Load initially at a slow rate, if possible by gravity.
- Check for leaks and that the correct tanks are being filled up.
- When rate is increased, check for leaks again and ensure that the ship/shore connections are checked for tightness
- Slowly increase the loading rate to maximum, continuously monitoring the manifold pressure.
- Deballasting operations are carried out concurrently

Topping Off

Completion of loading to the required ullage is called "topping off". The following must be carried out when topping off:

- When loading a "stagger" is built into the tanks by throttling the individual tank loading valves. This ensures that all tanks do not finish at the same time and gives adequate time between tank finishing.
- The ullage for the last tank to be topped off must take into account the amount of cargo in the line for draining purposes.
- Advise the shore when the final tanks are to be topped off and what the topping off sequence is to be
- Advise the shore in good time to reduce the loading rate sufficiently to permit effective control of the cargo flow.
- After topping off individual tanks the master valves must be shut to ensure segregation of cargo parcels.

- Always monitor ullages, including those of completed tanks, to ensure that spills and cargo overflow does not occur because of leaking valves.

- The number of valves to be closed during the topping off period must be reduced to a minimum.

- The tanker should not close all its valves against the flow of oil to prevent a pressure surge in the line.

- On completion of the final tank and line draining, the shore control valves must be closed before the ships' valves.

- After loading has been completed, a responsible ships' officer must check that all valves in the cargo system are closed, all appropriate tank openings are closed and that the pressure vacuum relief valves are correctly set.

Loaded Voyage

During the loaded voyage the cargo and associated spaces must be continuously monitored. The pressure/vacuum valves are usually set to automatic and, in the case of a low pressure alarm, the inert gas plant should be started to ensure a positive pressure of inert gas at all times. Some ships are equipped with a "top-up" inert gas plant for this purpose.

In the case of a double hull tanker, the double hull spaces must be monitored for hydrocarbon content at least once per week. During the loaded passage the ballast tanks should be sounded on a regular basis as a backup method of detecting any oil leakage.

Discharging

Before starting to discharge cargo, the ship and the terminal must formally agree that operations can be carried out safely. The appropriate section of the ship/shore safety checklist must be completed. The maximum discharge rates and manifold pressures must be agreed.

Inert Gas Operations

The inert gas system must be full operational and producing good quality inert gas of less than 5% oxygen at the start of the discharge operation.

Cargo discharge must not be started until:

- All relevant cargo tanks, including slop tanks, are common with the inert gas main

- All other cargo openings, including the vent valves are securely closed

- The inert gas plant is operating.

- The deck isolating valve is open and the fresh air intake is closed.

In the event of the failure of the inert gas system action must be taken to prevent any air being drawn into the tanks. All cargo and ballast operations must be stopped and the inert gas isolating valve must be closed and immediate action must be taken to repair the system.

Crude Oil Washing

On crude oil tankers that intend to carry out crude oil washing during discharge operations, the lines are pressure tested to their working pressure of 9-10 Kg/cm^2 and checked for leaks prior to arrival. The terminal is also informed about the need to crude oil wash and must allow this operation to be carried out, unless there is reasonable cause not to do so. Other ancillary systems are also tested at this stage and the results logged.

Discharging Operations

During discharge the following sequence of operations is usually carried out:

- The discharge plan is made and agreed by all parties.
- Complete the "line-up" and double check that the correct valves are open.
- The discharge plan must take into account any ballasting operations and, particularly on double hull tankers, the excessive free surface caused must be allowed for.
- The inert gas system must be in operation, as detailed previously.
- Shore valves must be fully open before opening the ships' manifold valves.
- Start at a slow rate and confirm with the terminal that the flow of cargo is being received in the correct tanks.
- Check for any leaks and then, on the agreement of the terminal, increase the cargo loading rate.
- If crude oil washing needs to be carried out the plan must be incorporated into the discharge plan and a responsible officer must monitor the operation.
- During discharge the tanker, in agreement with the terminal, must control the flow of cargo. The discharge rate must not be substantially changed without the agreement of the terminal.
- On completion of discharge the ship's deck cargo lines must be drained into an appropriate tank and then be discharged ashore or into a slop tank.

On completion of the discharging operation, and before the hoses or arms are disconnected, ships manifold valves and shore valves must be shut and the drain cocks at the vessels manifolds should be opened to drain into fixed drain tanks or portable drip trays. The contents of portable drip trays must be transferred to a slop tank or other safe receptacle.

Reference: ISGOTT, 4th edition 1996.

LIQUID CARGO CALCULATIONS

KEY POINTS

- Correct calculation of quantities are important to determine the cargo loaded and discharged

- The quantities have to be standardised to reference temperatures and densities

---

As oil expands when heated, an *Ullage space* is kept above the liquid level to allow for such expansion. *Ullage* is the measurement between the surface of a liquid cargo and the top of the tank. Sometimes the measurement may be up to the top of the ullage port, in which case the tank sounding or ullage tables will allow for this. The quantities loaded can be calculated by referring to the ullage section in the tank calibration tables.

In case of smaller ships, *soundings* may be taken instead of the ullage. A sounding is the measurement taken from the surface of the liquid to the bottom of the tank; i.e., the depth of liquid.

Both ullage measurements and soundings are affected by list and trim and tables that take account of this are used to correct the readings

The Relationship between Ullage & Sounding

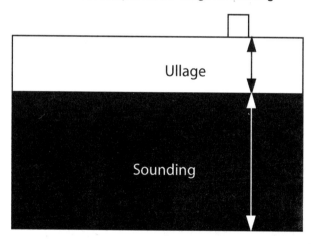

The expansion effect shows that the density of oil is dependent on the temperature. At higher temperatures the oil is less dense and occupies a greater space in the tanks.

The following is an example of a basic calculation to determine the weight of cargo to load and ullage at the time of loading,0. given the percentage expansion expected during the voyage:

A tank of Length 28m, Breadth 18.3m and Depth 12m is to be loaded with a vegetable oil of RD 0.830. The minimum ullage on passage is to be 0.27m. Assuming a 3% expansion on passage, calculate:-

1) The ullage on loading

2) The weight of oil loaded

Solution:

Final volume of oil: 28m x 18.3m x (12m -0.27m) = $6010.45\ m^3$

Volume of oil at loading = 6010.45 / 103 % (expansion) = $5835.39\ m^3$

Depth of oil on loading (sounding) = 5835.39 / (28 X 18.3) = 11.39 metres

Ullage on loading = depth of tank – sounding = I12 – 11.39 = **0.61 metres**

Weight of oil loaded = Volume X Relative Density =5835. 39m3 x 0.830

= 4843.4 tonnes

What complicates matters on board oil and product tankers is that the quantities calculated also include sediment and free water dissolved in the cargo. Also the cargo is loaded and discharged at different temperatures and this will affect the density. In order to avoid confusion the density is calculated at certain reference temperatures. Unfortunately different countries have different reference temperatures. The following are the reference temperatures used in oil trading:

- In the US   60 degrees F
- In Western Europe   15 degree C
- In Brazil and Eastern Europe   20 degree C

For volume measurement, two units exist. These are:

- The cubic meter (m^3) in metric countries
- The barrel (Bbl) in non-metric countries

It is customary to refer to volumes at the reference temperatures, as follows:

- US barrels @ 60 degree F or cubic meters @ 15 degree C

The following are the principal terms used in the measurement of oil cargoes:

Ullage hatch

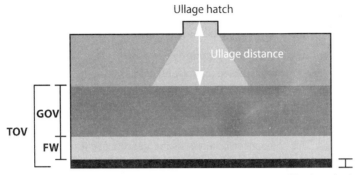

Hard-packed sediment

Total Observed Volume (TOV) – is the total volume of material measured in the tank including cargo (oil), free water (FW), entrained sediment and water (S&W) and sediment and scale as measured at ambient (observed) temperature and pressure.

Free water (FW) – the water layer existing as a separate phase normally detected by water paste or interface detector and usually settled at the bottom of the tank (depending on relative density of cargo).

Gross observed volume (GOV) - TOV less FW and bottom sediment, being the measured volume of oil and S&W at observed temperature and pressure. In practice the bottom sediment is difficult to quantify and is ignored.

Gross standard volume (GSV) - measured volume of oil and S&W at standard conditions of 15°C and atmospheric pressure. To obtain the GSV in practice the GOV is multiplied by a volume correction factor. This is obtained from standard tables like ASTM[1] table 54.

Net standard volume (NSV) - normally applicable to crude oil, NSV is the GSV minus sediment and water (S&W). For products, S&W is not normally deducted and is included in the cargo figures.

Total calculated volume (TCV) - total amount of oil, FW and S&W reported at standard temperature. In practice, TCV is the GSV plus the measured FW.

To calculate the amount of oil in a ships cargo tanks using a pre-determined temperature and the advised density, the volume correction factor (VCF) is determined from the American Society for Testing Materials (ASTM) and Institute of Petroleum (IP) *Petroleum Measurement Tables*. The GOV is multiplied by the

---

[1] *American Society for Testing Materials*

VCF to obtain the required GSV. Depending on the units in use, the VCF will standardise the oil volume to 15°C (m^3) or 60°F (US barrels).

Mainly, ASTM/IP tables 6, 24 and 54 are utilised to establish the VCF for a given density and temperature. Each of the tables is produced in three versions

- "A" version - for generalised crude oils.
- "B" version - for generalised (petroleum) products.
- "C" version - for individual and special applications.

Once the ship's loaded figures have been determined they must be compared to the shore figures. This comparison is known as the Vessel Load Ratio (VLR). Similarly, the Vessel Discharge Ratio (VDR) can also be determined at the discharge port. Using these figures the Vessel Experience Factor (VEF) can be determined. The VEF is the historical difference in ship and shore figures over a given period, usually 10 loadings. Using the VEF the chief officer can determine if the B/L quantity given is reliable. The VEF can change over a ships' lifetime due to the following:

- Change of trade
- Accumulation of sediments
- Descaling for dry docking
- Any structural alterations to the ship or the tanks

Each ship has a different VEF and it usually varies between -1% to +1% of the shore figures. The VEF of a vessel must be accurately determined and usually the Institute of Petroleum (IP) method is used. This involves taking the mean of the past Vessel Load Ratio (VLR) readings and deleting the values that do not fall within 0.3% of this mean. Another mean is then taken and this is the declared VEF.

Reference: Shipboard Petroleum Surveys, a Guide to Good Practice; Severn Anthony & the North of England P&I association, Anchorage Press (UK), 1995.

CHEMICAL CARGOES

KEY POINTS

- Chemical tankers have special regulations because of the hazards posed by the cargoes

- The International Code for the Construction and Equipment of Ships Carrying Chemical Cargoes in Bulk (IBC Code) and MARPOL contain these regulations.

Chemical cargoes carried in bulk can pose the following hazards:

- Toxicity
- Reactivity
- Corrosivity
- Flammability
- Pollution

IBC Code

The *International Code for the Construction and Equipment of Ships Carrying Chemical Cargoes in Bulk* (IBC Code) regulates the carriage of these potentially dangerous substances by sea and provides an international standard for the safe carriage in bulk of liquid chemicals.

The IBC Code applies to ships, regardless of size, engaged in the carriage of bulk cargoes of dangerous or noxious liquid chemical substances that have significant fire and other hazards in excess of those of petroleum cargoes.

The IBC Code applies to ships built on or after the 1st of July 1986. For ships built before 1986 another version of the code, called the *"BCH Code"*, applies. The substances to which the requirement of the Code applies are listed in Chapter 17 of the Code. Chapter 16 of the Code deals with the operational requirements of chemical tankers and includes safety features that are peculiar to them.

The IBC Code is divided as follows:

- Survival capability & tank location
- Ship arrangements
- Cargo containment
- Cargo transfer
- Construction materials
- Cargo temperature control
- Tank venting & gas-freeing arrangements

- Environmental control
- Electrical installations
- Fire protection & extinction
- Mechanical ventilation
- Instrumentation
- Personnel protection
- Special requirements
- Operational requirements
- Minimum requirements
- Transport of wastes

The basic philosophy of the Code is to class each chemical tanker by type, according to the degree of hazard presented by the products carried. The vessels are designed so as to minimise risk in the event of an incident of any kind, and will have sophisticated cargo monitoring systems and a high level of safety equipment.

Ship Types

The Codes consider the possibility that damage to the vessel from collision or grounding may result in an uncontrollable release of cargo to the atmosphere with resultant pollution, fire or toxic risks. To minimise this risk, vessels are classified into three types;

- Type 1 (offering the highest level of protection) for the most hazardous cargoes
- Type 2 intermediate protection
- Type 3 the lowest form of protection for the least harmful chemicals

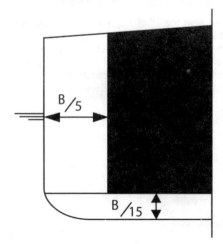

Type 1 Ship:

Designed for the carriage of chapter 17 products with severe environmental and safety hazards and which require maximum preventative measures to preclude an escape of the cargo. The design principle for these ships is that the cargo carrying compartments are located a minimum distance from the hull of the ship to guard against release due to collision or grounding. The tanks should be located at a distance not less than the breadth of the ship divided by 5, or 11.5 metres, whichever is less.

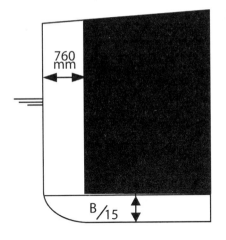

Type 2 Ship:

Designed for the carriage of chapter 17 products with appreciably severe environmental and safety hazards, which require significant preventative measures to preclude an escape of such cargo. The minimum distance of the cargo tanks are 760mm from the side shell plating and B/15 or 6 metres from the moulded bottom plating

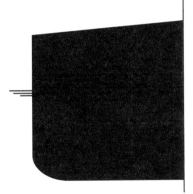

Type 3 Ship:

Designed to transport chapter 17 products with sufficiently severe environmental and safety hazards that they require a moderate degree of containment to increase survival capability in a damaged condition. There are no restrictions for the location of cargo tanks in a type 3 ship.

Certification

An *'International Pollution Prevention Certificate for the Carriage of Noxious Liquid Substances in Bulk (NLS Certificate)'* is required by ships engaged in the carriage of noxious liquid substances for bulk trading internationally. This includes offshore supply vessels carrying noxious liquid substances in cargo tanks as well as product carriers carrying noxious liquid cargoes.

Certificate of Fitness: All chemical tankers will be issued with a certificate of fitness that details the name and port of registry of the vessel, type of vessel, cargoes that can be carried, and the conditions of carriage of the cargoes. Chemical tankers issued with this will not require a NLS certificate as the certificate of fitness will be treated with the same force.

Cargoes

The majority of chemical cargoes carried by sea are transported in small quantities. Because of this chemical tankers are likely to have more than 30 different tanks. As many of these cargoes are not compatible with each other, the piping, ventilation and pumps are separate. Each tank usually contains a deepwell pump that is lubricated by the cargo itself. Tank coatings are also important as some cargoes can react with them. Newer ships have mainly stainless steel tanks as this does not react with any chemical. However, certain cargoes such as chlorides, fluorides, and acids may remove the anti corrosive properties of the steel. Other coatings include epoxy and zinc silicate. No matter what the coating of a tank is, none can ever be guaranteed against damage and they must be inspected regularly with any damage rectified immediately. Some epoxy coatings soften under the action of chemicals allowing the coating to absorb/retain some of the cargo. If this occurs the tank must be ventilated and washed before loading the next cargo. Due to the reactive nature of many cargoes an inhibitor may be added to stabilise the cargo.

Prior to loading a chemical cargo the ship's certificate of fitness must be consulted to determine if the ship is allowed to load that type of cargo. Then chapter 17 of the code must be consulted, which lists the minimum requirements for that type of cargo including ventilation, gauging, fire protection and other special requirements.

Finally other publications including the ships' *Procedures and Arrangements Manual* (P&A manual) will give ship specific requirements for that type of cargo. For tank cleaning requirements various industry guides exist including one published by the US Coast Guard that lists the different procedures to be followed in order to prepare tanks for the specified cargo. Before cargo transfer operations are commenced the *Ship/Shore Safety Checklist* is completed, including part "B", which deals specifically with chemical cargoes.

The '*International Chamber of Shipping' (ICS)* has published a guide called the '*Tanker Safety Guide' (Chemicals),* which contains general precautions and information regarding the risks and operational practices with such cargoes.

'*Material Safety Data Sheets' (MSDS)* provided by the shipper will detail the following information:

- Appearance
- Odour
- Hazards
- Emergency procedures
- Fire and explosive data
- Chemical data
- Reactivity information
- Health data
- Physical properties

- Handling and storage recommendations
- Manufacturers name
- Emergency contact number.

Disposal of tank washings are governed by MARPOL annex 2. According to the present regulations[1], cargoes are divided into four categories, A, B C and D, depending on the severity of the pollution hazard. Category A cargoes have the most severe pollution hazards and are banned from being discharged into the sea. Category D cargoes have the minimum hazards. Regulation 5 states the requirements for the discharge of category B, C and D and lists special areas where discharge of certain categories is forbidden. All ships to which annex II applies must carry and maintain a *Cargo Record Book*. This must be completed on a tank-to-tank basis, for all cargo handling, tank washing and ballast operations. Any discharges into the sea, for whatever reason, must also be recorded. The master and the officer in charge of the operation should sign each entry.

Inerting and Ventilation Requirements

All approved chemical tankers over 20,000 tonnes must have an inert gas plant. The venting system must be suitable for the cargo and must ensure that cargo vapour is neither able to accumulate on the decks or enter the accommodation. For this reason high velocity vents are used. Vapours must never be allowed to accumulate near sources of ignition.

Pipelines

Because of the complex nature of the cargoes carried pipeline systems can be very intricate and there may be as many as 50 manifolds, depending on the number of cargoes that the ship can carry. There are crossover valves and spool pieces that can be used to interconnect between different pipeline systems. Segregation of cargoes is important, not only for safety reasons but also for commercial purposes. Double valve segregation is the minimum required and in many cases completely separate and independent systems may be required.

Instrumentation and Personnel Protection

Modern chemical tankers have a centralised cargo control room and remote tank readings giving temperature, ullage, line pressure, valve positions, pump status and discharge rates. Valves, pumps and other cargo systems can be remotely operated from the cargo control room. For fire prevention purposes a fixed foam based system is carried which is capable of covering the entire cargo deck area and will last for at least 30 min at highest rate. For gas detection at least two

---

[1] *These regulations have been revised and the new requirements will enter into force from the 1st of January 2007. More information can be found on the IMO website, http://www.imo.org/*

instruments capable of detecting toxic & flammable concentrations must be carried, one of which may be fixed. These must be calibrated for specific vapours

For personal protection the following equipment is required:

- Chemical-resistant suits
- Face coverings, gas masks
- Stored in special lockers

Safety equipment sets (at least 3 sets carried)

- BA sets
- Protective clothing
- Fireproof, chemical resistant lifeline
- Explosion proof lamp

In addition the following equipment is carried for use in case of spillages or other emergencies:

- Stretchers
- Medical first-aid equipment
- Resuscitation equipment
- Antidotes for cargoes carried
- Decontamination showers and eyebaths on deck

Reference: IBC Code, ICS tanker Safety Guide (Chemical)

LIQUID GAS CARGOES

KEY POINTS

- Liquefied Petroleum Gas (LPG), Liquefied Chemical Gases and Liquefied Natural Gas (LNG) are transported by sea in specialised tankers.

- These cargoes are highly flammable and require special precautions

---

Liquefied gases transported by sea are mainly of three types:

- Liquefied Petroleum Gases (LPG)
- Liquefied Chemical Gases
- Liquefied Natural Gas (LNG)

Liquefied Petroleum Gases are mainly propane and butane or a mixture of the two. These are normally used as fuel for heating or cooking. Both Propane and Butane are heavier than air and are highly flammable.

Liquefied Chemical Gases are gases like Vinyl Chloride Monomer, Butadiene or Ammonia, which are manufactured gases.

Liquefied Natural Gas is methane or ethane, and these are used for heating and as fuel for power plants.

IGC Code

The '*International Code for the Construction and Equipment for Ships Carrying Liquefied Gases in Bulk*' *(IGC)* provides an international standard for the safe carriage by sea of liquefied gases (and other substances listed in the Code) in bulk. The purpose of the code is to minimize risks to the ships, their crews and the environment. The Code also prescribes the design and constructional standards of such ships and the equipment they should carry. The intent of this code is in line with that of the '*International Code for the Construction of Equipment of Ships Carrying Dangerous Chemicals in Bulk*' *(IBC Code)*. A ship complying with the IGC Code can be issued with an International Certificate of Fitness, which signifies that a minimum standard of constructional equipment and some operational safety has been achieved.

IGC Code

The IGC Code applies to gas carriers constructed on or after 1 July 1986. Gas carriers constructed before that date are recommended to comply with the requirements of the '*Code for the Construction and Equipment of Ships Carrying*

Liquefied Gases in Bulk' (GC Code) or the *'Code for Existing Ships Carrying Liquefied Gases in Bulk' (EGC Code).* The basic philosophy of the codes is to match a ship type with the hazards of the products transported.

<u>The Cargoes</u>

The IGC Code defines liquefied gases as

"Products having a vapour pressure exceeding 2.8 bar absolute at a temperature of 37.8 degrees Celsius and other products shown in Chapter 19 of the Code and carried in bulk."

In practical terms this means products that are gases at atmospheric pressure and ambient temperature. It is commercially and practically impossible to transport these substances in a gaseous state as, in case of LNG, 1 m^3 of LNG liquid would occupy 600m^3 as a gas. Therefore, the only practical way of transporting these substances in large amounts, is in the liquid form.

There are three ways in which these substances can be transported in a liquid form. They are:

Fully Pressurised: which is where the gas is loaded in a pressure vessel and allowed to evaporate. When the pressure inside the cylinder reaches the critical pressure[1] for the gas, the gas liquefies and remains in that state as long as the pressure is maintained. Most LPG and chemical gases can be transported in this form. LNG cannot be commercially transported in large quantities in this form as the critical pressure for LNG is in excess of 45 bars.

Typical working pressures are between 15 and 17 atmospheres. The drawback with this type of containment is the heavy construction of the cylindrical or spherical pressure tanks and, due to the shape of the tanks, a great deal of hull space is wasted.

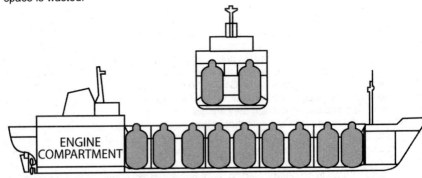

A fully pressurized LPG carrier

---

[1] *The pressure of a saturated vapour at the critical temperature (i.e. the pressure required to cause liquefaction at that temperature).*

Semi Refrigerated: LPG and chemical gases can be transported either in a pressurised or a refrigerated state. So in order to make the maximum use of this property and to ensure flexibility of carriage, many LPG and chemgas ships are built with pressure tanks and reliquefaction plants. The ships are so designed that they can carry their LPG cargoes either fully refrigerated, fully pressurised or a partial combination of the two.

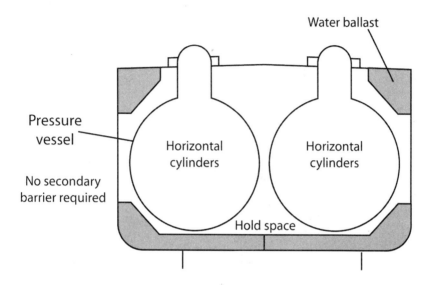

Fully Refrigerated: The other way to transport gases in their liquid form is to cool them down in shore tanks until the temperatures reach to just below their boiling point. In this way the liquefied gases can be transferred to the fully refrigerated ship, maintained at ship tank temperatures slightly above boiling point, and transported at near to atmospheric pressure. As the gas will boil off during the voyage, a means of controlling this boil off is required. On LPG vessels this is done by a reliquefaction plant, which reliquefies the boil off and returns liquid back to the tank. Since to reliquefy LNG very large pressures are required, and as the table of properties on the next page shows, LNG as a gas is lighter than air, on most LNG vessels the boil off is used as a fuel in the engine rooms. Recently there have been a few LNG vessels with on board reliquefaction plants but such ships are still rare.

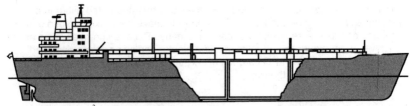

75,000 m³ FULLY REFRIGERATED LPG-CARRIER WITH SELF SUPPORTING PRISMATIC TANKS

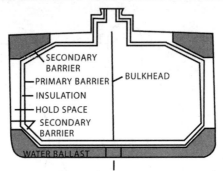

SELF SUPPORTING PRISMATIC TANK

FULLY REFRIGERATED TYPE "A" TANK

The following table shows the physical properties of commonly carried gases in the refrigerated condition:

Properties	Ammonia	n~Butane	Propane	Butadiene
Carriage Temperature °C (At Boiling Point)	-34	-1	-42.8	-5
Cargo Pressure kg/cm2 at Boiling Point	1.04	1.04	1.04	1.04
Specific Gravity of Liquid at STP	0.683	0.602	0.583	0.653
Vapour Density relative to Air at STP	0.587	2.09	1.55	1.88
Flammable limite % by Vol LFL-UFL	14~28	1.8~8.5	2.1~9.5	1.0~11.5
Flash Point °C	-57	-60	-105	-60
Ignition Temperature °C	635	365	470	415
Symbol	NH3	C4H10	C3H8	C4H6

<u>Ship Types</u>

The *IGC Code* specifies the following ship types:

TYPE "1G" SHIP

Designed to transport products indicated in Chapter 19 of the IGC Code which require *maximum* preventive measures to preclude the escape of such a cargo

[Chlorine, Ethylene Oxide, Methyl Bromide, Sulphur Dioxide]

TYPE "2G" SHIP

Designed to transport products indicated in Chapter 19 of the IGC Code which require *significant* preventive measures to preclude the escape of such a cargo

[Ethane, Methane (LNG), Ethylene]

TYPE "2PG" SHIP

Designed to transport products indicated in Chapter 19 of the IGC Code on a vessel of 150m or less in length which require *significant* preventive measures to preclude the escape of such cargo, and where the products are carried in independent type C tanks designed for a *MARVS*[2] of at least 7 bar and a cargo containment system design temperature of *-55 degrees* or above.

[Ammonia, Butadiene, Butane, Propane, etc]

TYPE "3G" SHIP

Designed to transport products indicated in Chapter 19 of the IGC Code, which require *moderate* preventive measures to preclude the escape of such cargo.

[Nitrogen, Refrigerant Gases (CFC)]

---

[2] *Maximum Allowable Relief Valve Setting*

Tank Location

Severe collisions or groundings could lead to cargo tank damage and uncontrolled release of the product. Such release could result in evaporation and dispersion of the product and, in some cases, could cause brittle fracture of the ship's hull. Hence, the tanks on board type 1 and type 2 gas tankers are located at stipulated minimum distances away from the ships hull and, in case of cargoes carried in the refrigerated form, a secondary barrier is required in most cases. In case of LNG, since cargoes are transported at very low temperatures (-160 deg C), it is important that any leakage does not come into contact with untreated surfaces as a brittle fracture and a subsequent hull failure will result.

Cargo Operations

Cargo operations on LPG and LNG tankers depend on the type of ship involved. Most LPG ships are provided with deepwell pumps, the very large LPG and LNG ships are provided with submerged pumps. Fully and semi refrigerated LPG ships are equipped with cargo compressors and reliquefaction plants to handle boil off. LNG vessels generally use the boil off gas as fuel to generate steam for the steam turbine plants or to power ancillary equipment like steam powered mooring winches.

In the case of a fully pressurised vessel carrying cargo at ambient temperatures, the loading and discharging process is more straightforward as the tanks are designed to take pressures of up to 15 to 17 atmospheres. The cargo can be discharged by pressurising the tanks and during loading the cargo is allowed to evaporate in the tank until the gas liquefies due to the increased pressure.

In the case of a semi-refrigerated vessel, if the cargo is carried in a refrigerated form, the cargo compressors are used to reliquefy the boil off and return cold liquid back to the tank. Since the tanks are designed to handle pressure of up to 9 bars (many having less than this at 4.5 or 7 bar capability), the cargo can be carried at intermediate temperatures and then cooled during the voyage if required.

In the case of fully refrigerated ships, including LNG vessels, the tanks are not designed to handle pressure more than 0.3 bar above the atmospheric pressure. Pressures are monitored very closely during the initial stages of the loading and in the case of refrigerated vessels the cargo compressors and the refrigeration system runs at full capacity.

The following flow chart illustrates a typical cycle of operation for a gas tanker equipped with a re-liquefaction plant from a dry-dock or repair yard back to a dry-dock or repair yard:

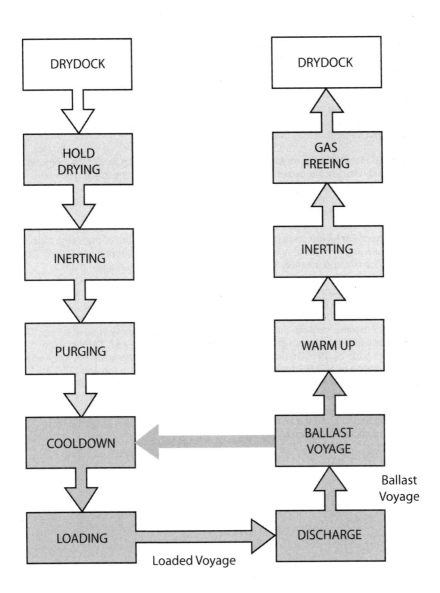

Hold Drying: On exiting a dry-dock or repair yard the tanks are full of air at ambient temperatures. Since the tanks will have to be cooled to accept the cargoes, it is necessary to reduce the dewpoint of the cargo so as to avoid the formation of ice and hydrates[3]. This is usually achieved by using an air drier.

Inerting: After the tank is full of dry air the inerting process can be started. LPG ships are equipped with an inert gas generator that can generate inert gas with an oxygen content of less than 2%.

Purging: Purging is the replacement of the inert gas with vapours of the cargo to be loaded. Usually the denser cargo gas is introduced from the loading line and the inert gas is returned to the shore via the vapour line (although this procedure has, in the past, often been carried out without a vapour return to shore and with the ship venting at sea).

Cooldown: Tanks are cooled down to reduce the temperature of the cargo tank prior to loading in order to minimise thermal stresses and over pressurisation from excessive vaporisation. On refrigerated ships the reliquefaction plant is used to draw vapours and return the cooled liquid via the spray line (see the following line diagram). On LNG vessels and ships that are on a dedicated route, with cargoes such as LPG or Ammonia, some amount of cargo called *heel* is retained on board from the last voyage and the tanks are kept cool for the next voyage. For initial cooling, cold liquid is introduced via the spray lines at a very slow rate while the thermal gradient inside the tank is monitored. Temperature gradients such as 12 to 15 degrees C may be experienced between the top and bottom plating of an LPG tank at this time, eg with -25C at the top and -37C at the bottom prior to loading a -42C propane. The inherent risk of vapour flashing over pressurisation when the initial cold propane liquid enters the bottom of the tank is likely to require immediate shut down and continued cooling / reliquefaction to bring the tank under pressure control. The line drawing taken shows a typical arrangement

---

[3] *Hydrates are slush like substances formed due to a reaction with cold LPG, these can block pumps and jam valves.*

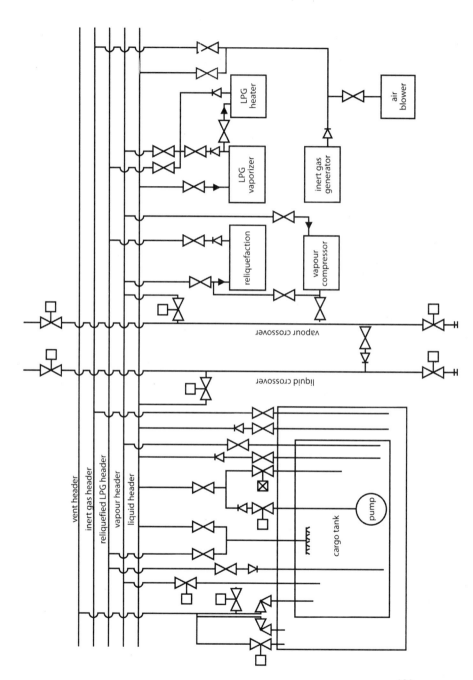

183

Loading: After cooldown the loading can commence, initially at a slow rate. The displaced vapours are either returned to shore or are reliquefied and sent back to the tank.

Loaded Passage: During the loaded passage the cargo pressures and temperatures are monitored and the cargo boil off reliquefied for quantity control. In the semi pressured ships with refrigeration capability the cargo liquid may even be may be cooled down for arrival, depending on the charter party requirements.

Ballast Voyage: During the ballast voyage on an LNG vessel the tanks are kept cool by extracting the boil off gas generated by the heel left on board. In the case of most other gas ships the ballast voyage may also involve preparation for a change of cargo.

Preparation for drydock: This involves warming up the tanks using vapour heaters and puddle heating coils if so equipped, then displacing the gas with inert gas in preparation for aerating and making tanks ready for inspection.

Safety and Personnel Protection

Due to the hazardous nature of the cargoes carried gas carriers are built to the highest safety standards and have alarms and instrumentation designed to be fail-safe. The basic principle of safe transportation of liquefied gas is not to allow a flammable atmosphere to form in the tanks at any time. This is achieved by carrying out all cargo operations in a closed cycle and keeping a positive pressure in the tanks at all times to prevent the entry of air and oxygen. At all times during cargo operations the space above the liquefied gas is filled with the vapour of the cargo. Since the atmosphere is over rich and there is no oxygen present combustion cannot occur.

The ships are equipped with various safety and monitoring systems in order to avoid any untoward incidents. Emergency Shutdown systems (ESD) are linked to high level alarms, tank pressure alarms and heat sensors and on activation shut down the pumps and associated systems and close the manifold valves. On LNG ships the ship ESD system is linked to the shore ESD system so as to coordinate shutdown and avoid pressure surges. Variations of this can be found at some ship/shore interface locations dealing with other gas ship types and it has been recommended that all such locations will adopt this practice.

The ship is divided into gas dangerous and gas safe areas (see diagram below) and fixed gas monitoring equipment is installed in the gas dangerous areas to detect any leaks. The interbarrier spaces (spaces between the tanks and the hull) are filled with inert gas and fixed gas detectors and pressure detectors also monitor these spaces.

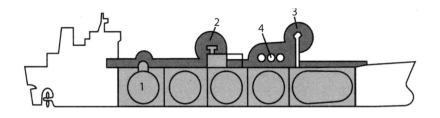

■ Gas dangerous zones	
■ Gas dangerous spaces	1 Cargo Tank
□ Gas safe spaces and zones	2 Ventilation outlet from compressor room
	3 Vent mast outlet
	4 Cargo pipelines

For personnel protection water spray systems are provided along with fixed and portable gas detectors and chemical suits, eye baths and decontamination showers. For cargo related fire fighting on gas ships, dry powder is used. Fixed monitors are provided and a supply of dry powder is available to fight fires on deck. Additional medical equipment is also provided for treatment in case of any exposure to the cargo.

Reference: Liquefied Gas Handling Principles on Ships and in Terminals - 3rd edition and SIGTTO website (www.sigtto.org)

<u>ANNEXES</u>

Principles and Operational Guidance for Deck Officers in Charge of a Watch In Port

Recommendations and Principles and Operational Guidance for Deck Officers in Charge of a Watch in Port

This recommendation applies to ships that are safely moored or safely anchored under normal circumstances in port and where the master has decided in the prevailing conditions that a navigational watch need not be kept.

Watch arrangements

1. Arrangements for keeping a watch when the ship is in port should;
   a. Ensure the safety of life, ship, cargo and port
   b. Observe international, national and local rules.
   c. Maintain order and the normal routine of the ship.

2. The ship's master should decide the composition and duration of the watch, depending on the conditions of mooring, type of ship and character of duties.

3. A qualified deck officer should be in charge of the watch, except in ships under 500 GRT not carrying dangerous cargo, in which case the master may appoint whoever has appropriate qualifications to keep the watch in port.

4. The necessary equipment should be so arranged as to provide for efficient watch keeping.

Taking Over the Watch

5. The officer of the watch should not hand over the watch to the relieving officer if he has any reason to believe that the latter is obviously not capable of carrying out his duties effectively, in which case he should notify the master accordingly.

6. The relieving officer should be informed of the following by the officer being relieved;
   a. The depth of water at the berth ship draft, the level and time of high and low waters, fastening of the moorings, arrangement of anchors and the slip of the chain and other features of mooring important for the safety of the ship; status main engines and availability for emergency use.
   b. All work to be performed on board the ship, the nature, amount and disposition of cargo loaded or remaining or any residue on board after unloading the ship.
   c. The level of water in bilges and ballast tanks.
   d. The signals or lights being exhibited
   e. The number of crew members required to be onboard and the presence of any other person on board.
   f. The state of fire fighting appliances.

g. Any special port regulations.
h. The masters standing and special orders
i. The lines of communication that are available between the ship and the dock staff of port authorities in the event of an emergency arising or assistance being required.
j. Other circumstances of importance to the safety of the ship and protection of the environment from pollution.

7. The relieving officer should satisfy himself that;
    a. Fastenings of moorings or anchor chain are adequate
    b. The appropriate signals or lights are properly hoisted and exhibited.
    c. Safety measures and fire protection regulations are being maintained.
    d. He is aware of the nature of any hazardous or dangerous cargo being loaded or discharged and the appropriate action in the event of any spillage or fire
    e. No external conditions or circumstances imperil the ship and that his own ship does not imperil others.

8. If at the moment of handing over the watch, an important operation is being performed it should be concluded by the officer being relieved, except when ordered otherwise by the master.

Keeping a Watch

9. The officer of the watch should
    a. Make rounds to inspect the ship at appropriate intervals
    b. Pay particular attention to;
        i. The conditions and fastening of the gangway, anchor chain or moorings, especially at the turn of the tide or in berth with a large rise and fall and if necessary take measures to ensure that they are in normal working condition
        ii. The draft, under keel clearance and the state of the ship to avoid dangerous listing or trim during cargo handling or ballasting
        iii. The state of the weather and sea.
        iv. Observance of all regulations concerning safety precautions and fire protection
        v. Water level in bilges and tanks.
        vi. All person on board and their location especially those in remote or enclosed spaces.
        vii. The exhibition of any signals or lights
    c. In bad weather or on receiving a storm warning, take the necessary measures to protect the ship, personnel and cargo
    d. Take every precaution to prevent pollution of the environment by his own ship
    e. In an emergency threatening the safety of the ship, raise the alarm, inform the master, take all possible measures to prevent any damage to the ship and if necessary, request assistance from the shore authorities or neighbouring ships

f. Be aware of the state of stability so that in the event of fire, the shore fire fighting authority may be advised of the approximate quantity of water that can be pumped on board without endangering the ship.

g. Offer assistance to ships or persons in distress.

h. Take necessary precautions to prevent accidents or damage when propellers are to be turned.

i. Enter in the appropriate log book, all important events affecting the ship.

"Principles for the keeping of a safe watch in port" is based on the withdrawn M Notice 1016, however the guidance contained within it remains a valuable and valid reference source.

Maritime and Coastguard Agency

Ro-Ro Ships
Vehicle Decks - Accidents to Personnel, Passenger Access and the Carriage of Motor Vehicles

Notice to owners, managers, operators, masters, officers, ratings and shippers of vehicles

(This note supersedes Merchant Shipping Notice No. M.1433 and M.1507)

Summary

This guidance highlights the dangers to passengers and crew from moving vehicles during loading and unloading operations on board ro-ro ships. It also contains the following interpretation of United Kingdom and international regulations:

1) Interpretation of SOLAS 1974, Chapter II-1 Regulation 20.3 given at paragraph 3, concerning access by passengers to the enclosed vehicle decks of ro-ro ships, including permissible exceptions to that regulation; and

2) lists minimum safety conditions for fuel carried in the tanks of motor vehicles and other specified articles and materials when carried in connection with a vehicle operation or business, which are considered necessary for exclusion from "dangerous goods" requirements.

This guidance is applicable to all United Kingdom ships and all ships within United Kingdom ports.

1. Introduction

1.1 A vehicle deck is a potentially dangerous environment due to congestion and the movement of vehicles, many with flammable fuel in their tanks or carried on the vehicles. These conditions have resulted in accidents and at least one death of a crew member. It is clearly desirable that the length of time that passengers spend on a vehicle deck should be kept to a minimum and that access by crew should be restricted to those who need to be there. The purpose of this Guidance Note is to remind owners, operators and seafarers of the dangers involved and to give advice on the precautions required.

2. Statutory Requirements

2.1 Employers have a general duty to ensure, so far as is reasonably practicable, the health and safety of employees and other persons on board ship as required by the Merchant Shipping and Fishing Vessels (Health and Safety at Work) Regulations 1997, as amended.

2.2 More particularly, the Merchant Shipping (Safe Movement on Board Ship) Regulations 1988, as amended, require that the employer and Master shall ensure that safe means of access is provided and maintained to any place on the ship to which a person may be expected to go. Additionally, the employer

1

and Master are required to ensure that danger from the use or movement of vehicles and mobile lifting appliances is so far as is reasonably practicable prevented. Similar provisions are contained in the Health and Safety (The Docks) Regulations 1988.

2.3 When vehicles, caravans, boats, etc. are carried in accordance with the provisions of this Guidance Note the goods they are carrying (limited to those goods specified in this Guidance Note) are not classified as dangerous goods. When these conditions are not complied with, the requirements of the Merchant Shipping (Dangerous Goods and Marine Pollutants) Regulations 1997 may apply to both the vehicles and freight carried by them.

3. Passenger Access to Vehicle Decks

3.1 The SOLAS Convention Chapter II-1 Reg 20-3, requires that "In all ro-ro passenger ships, the master or the designated officer shall ensure that, without the expressed consent of the master or the designated officer, no passengers are allowed access to an enclosed ro-ro deck when the ship is underway." Except for access in emergency situations, consent should be limited to the following circumstances:

.1 in order to facilitate the ordered movement of passengers towards the end of a voyage and only if the master considers it to be safe, passengers may be allowed access to the vehicle deck provided the ship is not more than two ship's lengths from its berth;

.2 individual passengers under special circumstances and only for brief periods when they should be accompanied by a crew member;

.3 people with disabilities that seriously affect their mobility, where special arrangements have been made prior to the journey; and

.4 ferries on very short crossings where all vehicles are stowed on an open deck in accordance with provisions agreed between the ferry operator and the Maritime and Coastguard Agency (MCA).

4. The Dangers of Accidents

4.1 The speed of cargo operations combined with large vehicles being manoeuvred in a confined space is clearly hazardous to personnel.

4.2 In recent accidents, seafarers have been killed or injured during cargo operations involving flat-bed trailers or similar being driven by shore-personnel, despite the presence of signalers and ship's staff.

4.3 Many of the vehicles now being loaded on ships are larger than was envisaged when the ships were designed and built and are of such design that the view from the driving position, particularly when manoeuvering in reverse, is severely limited. This increases the hazards due to the limited walkway space available.

4.4 A number of cases of petrol spillage from vehicles carried on ro-ro ferries have been reported. These cases and others involving the leakage of flammable liquids and gases could have given rise to serious incidents.

5. Safety Provisions

5.1 In all cases the most effective method of ensuring the safety of personnel is to keep people and moving vehicles apart by preventing access to the decks during cargo operations.

5.2 During normal operations this is impracticable but nevertheless the fewer people that have access to the decks the less likelihood there is of accidents occurring, especially to those that do not need to be on the vehicle decks during cargo operations. Personnel are reminded that if access to these decks is necessary only the marked and authorised routes on decks and vehicle ramps should be used.

5.3 Personnel that are required to be on the vehicle decks as part of their job should be made aware of the dangers and the systems in operation for their safety, including the wearing of high-visibility garments. Consideration should also be given to the need for the person in charge of cargo operations to communicate with drivers of vehicles and in particular the need to alert drivers quickly to any dangerous situation that may be developing.

5.4 Personnel involved in controlling vehicles should avoid standing directly between the vehicle being moved and any obstruction and should stand to the side. The position chosen should, where possible, be such that the risk of being trapped between the moving vehicle and an obstruction is minimised. Safety will also be enhanced by remaining in the driver's line of sight, always having regard to the location of the driving position of the vehicle in different countries. Personnel supervising vehicle deck operations are reminded that dangers to personnel are significantly increased when vehicles are driven on board at excessive speed.

5.5 Ship's staff should exercise special care where persons unaccustomed to vehicle deck operations require access to the deck. Car drivers and coach passengers are unlikely to be familiar with their surroundings or the operations involved, making them particularly vulnerable to the dangers.

5.6 Well illuminated, permanently marked and clearly signposted walkways should be provided for all those who require access to the vehicle decks both during cargo operations and when the ship is at sea. In addition, suitable barriers should be in place adjacent to doorways and exits that open directly onto the vehicle decks to prevent any person inadvertently walking straight onto the deck and into the path of a moving vehicle. Other measures such as deck mounted kerbs that force vehicles to maintain a safe distance from doorways and exits are also recommended.

5.7 Owners and operators are also strongly recommended to have suitable notices warning of the dangers at all locations where there is access to vehicle decks.

6. **Petrol and diesel in the tanks of motor vehicles**

6.1 When vehicles are carried in cargo spaces which, under Merchant Shipping legislation or by equivalent arrangements agreed with the MCA, are suitable for the carriage of motor vehicles with fuel in their tanks for their own propulsion, it is important to ensure that on each vehicle:

.1 the tank is not so full as to create a possibility of spillage; and

.2 the ignition is switched off.

6.2 Spare cans of petrol should not be carried.

6.3 Occasionally, machinery such as a mobile generator carried on a vehicle, is offered for shipment. These have fuel tanks and batteries and present the same hazard as motor vehicles; they should be carried under the same conditions as motor vehicles.

7. **Motor vehicles propelled by liquefied petroleum gas (LPG) or Natural gas, compressed or refrigerated (LNG).**

7.1 Motor vehicles propelled by LPG should have gas storage and associated systems built to standards equivalent to the Road Vehicles (Construction and Use) Regulations 1986, as amended.

7.2 Motor vehicles propelled by liquefied petroleum gas (LPG) or liquified natural gas (LNG), may be carried in the cargo spaces referred to in paragraph 6.1 provided:

.1 the ignition is switched off; and

.2 the gas is contained in a cylinder or cylinders with valves which should be closed when the vehicle is in position on board ship.

7.3 Only properly piped and fitted cylinders should be allowed. All cylinders of LPG or LNG should be properly secured.

8. **Gas cylinders in boats, caravans and in other vehicles where the gas is used solely in connection with its operation or business.**

8.1 Steps should be taken to ensure that all cylinders are declared by passengers to the ship's officer in charge of loading and the following conditions should apply:

.1 the maximum number of cylinders carried should be three, except in the case of small expendable cartridges hermetically sealed and packed in an outer container, when up to twelve may be carried;

3

.2 all cylinders should be adequately secured against movement of the ship;

.3 the supply should be shut off at the cylinders during the entire voyage; and

.4 leaking and inadequately secured or connected cylinders should be refused for shipment.

9. Operational procedures

9.1 To guard against the possibility of incidents involving the spillage of fuel the following precautions should be observed:

.1 any vehicle showing visual signs of an overfilled tank should not be loaded;

.2 passengers should not be allowed access to vehicle decks once vessels are underway, (see paragraph 3 above and when dangerous goods are carried see Section 17.4 of the International Maritime Dangerous Goods Code);

.3 conspicuous "No Smoking" notices should be posted, together with notices warning against engines being started before doors leading to ramps are opened and a crew member should be positioned to instruct passengers accordingly;

.4 a fire patrol should be maintained on vehicle decks during the passage unless a fixed fire detection system and a television surveillance system are provided;

.5 any spillage of petrol should be quickly cleaned up; sand boxes, drip trays and mopping up equipment should be provided for use on each vehicle deck;

.6 a high standard of crew fire drill should be maintained;

.7 in the case of specially constructed ships where there are vehicle decks dedicated to the carriage of motor vehicles in a drive-on/drive-off condition, allowance should be made for the fact that flammable vapours and noxious fumes are evolved during the process of shipment. To ensure adequate air circulation, ventilation systems serving the vehicle decks should be in operation during any loaded voyage. When vehicles are being loaded or unloaded the number of air changes may need to be increased to ensure that any concentration of vapours or noxious fumes does not become a hazard to health[1].

MSASD, Cargoes and MSOS
Marine Safety Agency
Spring Place
105 Commercial Road
Southampton
SO15 1EG

Tel: 01703 329 184 or 01703 329 225
Fax: 01703 329 204

MS 116_031_00

April 1998

© Crown Copyright 1998

DETR
ENVIRONMENT
TRANSPORT
REGIONS

An executive agency of the Department of the Enviroment, Transport and the Regions

[1] The Control of Substances Hazardous to Health Regulations 1988 (COSHH) apply to exhaust emissions and to the clearance of spillage in UK ports.

MARINE SAFETY AGENCY

Code of Safe Practice for Solid Bulk Cargoes (BC Code) : 1996 Amendment

Carriage of Coal Cargoes

Notice to operators, shipowners, charterers, managers, masters, ship's officers and shippers.

Summary :

This Marine Guidance Note draws attention to the important changes to the provisions on the carriage of coal cargoes in the 1996 amendment of the BC Code.

1. The 1996 amendment of the IMO : Code of Safe Practice for Solid Bulk Cargoes (BC Code) includes changes to the individual schedule for Coal in Appendix B and a new Appendix G on Procedures for gas monitoring of Coal Cargoes.

2. Coal cargoes may emit methane gas which is flammable. A methane/air mixture containing between 5% and 16% methane constitutes an explosive atmosphere that can be ignited by sparks or naked flame. Accumulation of this gas in the hold may also result in leakage into adjacent spaces. Normally all holds should be surface ventilated for the first 24 hours after departure from the loading port. If the methane concentration is found to be acceptably low at the end of this period the ventilators are closed. On the other hand, if the concentration of methane as measured is over 20% of the LEL (Lower Explosive Limit), adequate surface ventilation is to be maintained to reduce the concentration.

3. Some coals may be subject to self-heating. To control the start of potential self-heating the hatches are kept closed and surface ventilation is limited to the absolute minimum time to remove any accumulated methane. Any self-heating is indicated by increasing concentration of carbon monoxide in the hold.

4. The Code requires that prior to departure the cargo should be trimmed reasonably level to the boundaries of the cargo space to avoid the formation of gas pockets and to prevent air permeating the body of the coal. This aspect is sometimes ignored in the rush to sail from the port and untrimmed holds can contribute to self-heating during the voyage.

5. Ships engaged in the carriage of coal should carry on board an instrument for measuring methane, oxygen and carbon monoxide gas concentrations so that the atmosphere within the cargo space may be monitored. The ships should also be provided with equipment suitable for taking a sample to be read by the instrument and sampling points sited on the hatch coamings as high as possible in accordance with Appendix G of the BC Code.

6. The individual schedule for coal provides detailed guidance on handling of coal cargoes and the Appendix G on procedures for monitoring the gases. These are annexed to this note for ready reference.

7. Safety, when carrying coal cargoes, cannot be taken for granted. The equipment should be serviced and instruments

calibrated at regular intervals in accordance with the manufacturer's instructions and the ship staff trained in the use of the equipment. Regular gas monitoring of the cargoes provides the necessary information for detecting at an early stage potential problems and following appropriate procedures for safe carriage.

8. With the exception of ships engaged on coastal voyages of short duration which need not be provided with carbon monoxide gas monitoring equipment, all ships engaged in the trade should be provided with the equipment and fitted out as required by the Code as soon as possible. Shipowners, masters and shippers are requested to note the changes and to observe the new provisions of the Code in cargo operations.

9. The Code of Safe Practice for Solid Bulk Cargoes (BC Code) is a publication of the International Maritime Organization and can be obtained from the International Maritime Organization, 4 Albert Embankment, London SE1 7SR.

MSAS D
Marine Safety Agency
Spring Place
105 Commercial Road
Southampton SO15 1EG

Tel 01703 329176
Fax 01703 329204

February 1998

MS54/02/08

© Crown Copyright 1998

DETR
ENVIRONMENT
TRANSPORT
REGIONS

An executive agency of the Department of the Enviroment, Transport and the Regions

COAL*

(See also appendix A)

BC No.	IMO class	MFAG table no.	Approximate stowage factor (m³/t)	EmS no.
010	MHB	311,616†	0.79 to 1.53	B14

Properties and characteristics

1 Coals may emit methane, a flammable gas. A methane/air mixture containing between 5% and 16% methane constitutes an explosive atmosphere which can be ignited by sparks or naked flame, e.g. electrical or frictional sparks, a match or lighted cigarette. Methane is lighter than air and may, therefore, accumulate in the upper region of the cargo space or other enclosed spaces. If the cargo space boundaries are not tight, methane can seep through into spaces adjacent to the cargo space.

2 Coals may be subject to oxidation, leading to depletion of oxygen and an increase in carbon dioxide in the cargo space (see also section 3 and appendix F).

3 Some coals may be liable to self-heating that could lead to spontaneous combustion in the cargo space. Flammable and toxic gases, including carbon monoxide, may be produced. Carbon monoxide is an odourless gas, slightly lighter than air, and has flammable limits in air of 12% to 75% by volume. It is toxic by inhalation, with an affinity for blood haemoglobin over 200 times that of oxygen.

4 Some coals may be liable to react with water and produce acids which may cause corrosion. Flammable and toxic gases, including hydrogen, may be produced. Hydrogen is an odourless gas, much lighter than air, and has flammable limits in air of 4% to 75% by volume.

Segregation and stowage requirements

1 Boundaries of cargo spaces where materials are carried should be resistant to fire and liquids.

2 Coals should be "separated from" goods of classes 1 (division 1.4), 2, 3, 4, and 5 in packaged form (see IMDG Code) and "separated from" solid bulk materials of classes 4 and 5.1.

3 Stowage of goods of class 5.1 in packaged form or solid bulk materials of class 5.1 above or below a coal cargo should be prohibited.

4 Coals should be "separated longitudinally by an intervening complete compartment or hold from" goods of class 1 other than division 1.4.

Note: For the interpretation of the segregation terms see paragraph 9.3.3.

---

* For comprehensive information on transport of any material listed, refer to sections 1-10 of this Code.

† Refer to paragraph 6.1.1 (Asphyxia) of the MFAG.

General requirements for all coals

1   Prior to loading, the shipper or his appointed agent should provide in writing to the master the characteristics of the cargo and the recommended safe handling procedures for loading and transport of the cargo. As a minimum, the cargo's contract specifications for moisture content, sulphur content and size should be stated, and especially whether the cargo may be liable to emit methane or self-heat.

2   The master should be satisfied that he has received such information prior to accepting the cargo. If the shipper has advised that the cargo is liable to emit methane or self-heat, the master should additionally refer to the "Special precautions".

3   Before and during loading, and while the material remains on board, the master should observe the following:

.1   All cargo spaces and bilge wells should be clean and dry. Any residue of waste material or previous cargo should be removed, including removable cargo battens, before loading.

.2   All electrical cables and components situated in cargo spaces and adjacent spaces should be free from defects. Such cables and electrical components should be safe for use in an explosive atmosphere or positively isolated.

.3   The ship should ▷ be suitably fitted and ◁ carry on board appropriate instruments for measuring the following without requiring entry in the cargo space:

.3.1   concentration of methane in the atmosphere;

.3.2   concentration of oxygen in the atmosphere;

.3.3   concentration of carbon monoxide in the atmosphere; ▷ and ◁

.3.4   pH value of cargo hold bilge samples ▷.◁

These instruments should be regularly serviced and calibrated. Ship personnel should be trained in the use of such instruments. ▷ Details of gas measurement procedures are given in appendix G. ◁

▷.4   It is recommended that means be provided for measuring the temperature of the cargo in the range 0°C to 100°C. Such arrangements should enable the temperature of the coal to be measured while being loaded and during the voyage without requiring entry into the cargo space. ◁

▷.5◁   The ship should carry on board the self-contained breathing apparatus required by SOLAS regulation II-2/17. The self-contained breathing apparatus should be worn only by personnel trained in its use (see also section 3 and appendix F).

▷.6◁   Smoking and the use of naked flames should not be permitted in the cargo areas and adjacent spaces and appropriate warning notices should be posted in conspicuous places. Burning, cutting, chipping, welding or other sources of ignition should not be permitted in the vicinity of cargo spaces or in other adjacent spaces, unless the space has been properly ventilated and the methane gas measurements indicate it is safe to do so.

▷.7◁   The master should ensure that the coal cargo is not stowed adjacent to hot areas.

▷.8 ◁ Prior to departure, the master should be satisfied that the surface of the material has been trimmed reasonably level to the boundaries of the cargo space to avoid the formation of gas pockets and to prevent air from permeating the body of the coal. Casings leading into the cargo space should be adequately sealed. The shipper should ensure that the master receives the necessary co-operation from the loading terminal (see also section 5).

▷.9 ◁ The atmosphere in the space above the cargo in each cargo space should be regularly monitored for the presence of methane, oxygen and carbon monoxide. ▷ Details of gas monitoring procedures are given in appendix G. ◁ Records of these readings should be maintained. The frequency of the testing should depend upon the information provided by the shipper and the information obtained through the analysis of the atmosphere in the cargo space. ▷ ◁

▷.10 Unless expressly directed otherwise, all holds should be surface ventilated for the first 24 hours after departure from the loading port. During this period, one measurement should be taken from one sample point per hold.

If after 24 hours the methane concentrations are at an acceptably low level, the ventilators should be closed. If not, they should remain open until acceptably low levels are obtained. In either event, measurements should be continued on a daily basis.

If significant concentrations of methane subsequently occur in unventilated holds, the appropriate special precautions as described in section 2.2.1 should apply. ◁

▷.11 ◁ The master should ensure, as far as possible, that any gases which may be emitted from the materials do not accumulate in adjacent enclosed spaces.

▷.12 ◁ The master should ensure that enclosed working spaces, e.g. store-rooms, carpenter's shop, passage ways, tunnels, etc., are regularly monitored for the presence of methane, oxygen and carbon monoxide. Such spaces should be adequately ventilated.

▷.13 ◁ Regular hold bilge testing should be systematically carried out. If the pH monitoring indicates that a corrosion risk exists, the master should ensure that all ▷ ◁ bilges are kept dry during the voyage in order to avoid possible accumulation of acids on tank tops and in the bilge system.

▷.14 ◁ If the behaviour of the cargo during the voyage differs from that specified in the cargo declaration, the master should report such differences to the shipper. Such reports will enable the shipper to maintain records on the behaviour of the coal cargoes, so that the information provided to the master can be reviewed in the light of transport experience.

▷.15 ◁ The Administration may approve alternative requirements to those recommended in this schedule.

Special precautions

1   *Coals emitting methane*

If the shipper has advised that the cargo is liable to emit methane or analysis of the atmosphere in the cargo space indicates the presence of methane ▷ in excess of 20% of the lower explosion limit (LEL) ◁, the following additional precautions should be taken:

.1   Adequate surface ventilation should be maintained. On no account should air be directed into the body of the coal as air could promote self-heating.

.2   Care should be taken to vent any accumulated gases prior to removal of the hatch covers or other openings for any reason, including unloading. Cargo hatches and other openings should be opened carefully to avoid creating sparks. Smoking and the use of naked flame should be prohibited.

.3   Personnel should not be permitted to enter the cargo space or enclosed adjacent spaces unless the space has been ventilated and the atmosphere tested and found to be gas-free and to have sufficient oxygen to support life. If this is not possible, emergency entry into the space should be undertaken only by trained personnel wearing self-contained breathing apparatus, under the supervision of a responsible officer. In addition, special precautions to ensure that no source of ignition is carried into the space should be observed (see also section 3 and appendix F).

.4   The master should ensure that enclosed working spaces, e.g. store-rooms, carpenter's shops, passage ways, tunnels, etc., are regularly monitored for the presence of methane. Such spaces should be adequately ventilated and, in the case of mechanical ventilation, only equipment safe for use in an explosive atmosphere should be used. Testing is especially important prior to permitting personnel to enter such spaces or energizing equipment within those spaces.

2   *Self-heating coals*

.1   If the shipper has advised that the cargo is liable to self-heat, the master ▷ should ◁ seek confirmation that the precautions intended to be taken and the procedures intended for monitoring the cargo during the voyage are adequate.

.2   If the cargo is liable to self-heat or analysis of the atmosphere in the cargo space indicates an increasing concentration of carbon monoxide ▷ ◁, then the following additional precautions should be taken:

.2.1   The hatches should be closed immediately after completion of loading in each cargo space. The hatch covers can also be additionally sealed with a suitable sealing tape. Surface ventilation should be limited to the ▷ absolute minimum time ◁ necessary to remove ▷ methane ◁ which may have accumulated. Forced ventilation should not be used. On no account should air be directed into the body of the coal as air could promote self-heating.

.2.2   Personnel should not be allowed to enter the cargo space, unless they are wearing self-contained breathing apparatus and access is critical to the safety of the ship or safety of life. The self-contained breathing apparatus should be worn only by personnel trained in its use (see also section 3 and appendix F).

.2.3   When required by the competent authority, the ▷ carbon monoxide concentration ◁ in each cargo space should be measured at regular time intervals to detect self-heating.

6

▷.2.4   If at the time of loading, when the hatches are open, the temperature of the coal exceeds 55°C, expert advice should be obtained. ◁

▷.2.5 ◁ If ▷ ◁ the carbon monoxide level is increasing ▷ steadily ◁ , a potential ▷ self-heating ◁ may be developing. The cargo space should be completely closed down and all ventilation ceased. The master should seek expert advice immediately ▷ ◁ . Water should not be used for cooling the material or fighting coal cargo fires at sea, but may be used for cooling the boundaries of the cargo space.

▷.2.6   Information to be passed to owners.

The most comprehensive record of measurements will always be the log used to record daily results. The coal cargo monitoring log for the voyage should be faxed, or the appropriate content should be telexed to the vessel's owners.

The following minimum information is essential if an accurate assessment of the situation is to be achieved.

(a)   identity of the holds involved; monitoring results covering carbon monoxide, methane and oxygen concentrations;

(b)   if available, temperature of coal, location and method used to obtain results;

(c)   time gas samples taken (monitoring routine);

(d)   time ventilators opened/closed;

(e)   quantity of coal in hold(s) involved;

(f)   type of coal as per shipper's declaration, and any special precautions indicated on declaration;

(g)   date loaded, and ETA at intended discharge port (which should be specified); and

(h)   comments or observations from the ship's master. ◁

PROCEDURES FOR GAS MONITORING OF COAL CARGOES

G.1   Observations

Carbon monoxide monitoring, when conducted in accordance with the following recommendations, will provide a reliable early indication of self-heating within a coal cargo. This allows preventive action to be considered without delay. A steady rise in the level of carbon monoxide detected within a hold is conclusive indication that self-heating is taking place.

All vessels engaged in the carriage of coal should carry on board an instrument for measuring methane, oxygen and carbon monoxide gas concentrations (general requirements for all coals, section 3.3 in the coal entry, appendix B), so that the atmosphere within the cargo space may be monitored. This instrument should be regularly serviced and calibrated in accordance with the manufacturer's instructions. When properly maintained and operated, this instrument will provide reliable data about the atmosphere within the cargo space. Care needs to be exercised in interpreting methane measurements carried out in the low oxygen concentrations often found in unventilated cargo holds. The catalytic sensors normally used for the detection of methane rely on the presence of sufficient oxygen for accurate measurement. This phenomenon does not affect the measurement of carbon monoxide, or measurement of methane by infrared sensor. Further guidance may be obtained from the instrument manufacturer.

G.2   Sampling and measurement procedure

G.2.1   *Equipment*

An instrument is required which is capable of measuring methane, oxygen and carbon monoxide concentrations. The instrument should be fitted with an aspirator, flexible connection and a length of tubing to enable a representative sample to be obtained from within the square of the hatch. Stainless steel tubing approximately 0.5 m in length and 6 mm nominal internal diameter with an integral stainless steel threaded collar is preferred. The collar is necessary to provide an adequate seal at the sampling point.

A suitable filter should be used to protect the instrument against the ingress of moisture as recommended by the manufacturer. The presence of even a small amount of moisture will compromise the accuracy of the measurement.

Siting of sampling points

In order to obtain meaningful information about the behaviour of coal in a hold, gas measurements should be made via one sample point per hold. To ensure flexibility of measurement in adverse weather, however, two sample points should be provided per hold, one on the port side and one on the starboard side of the hatch cover (refer to figure G.2.7). Measurement from either of these locations is satisfactory.

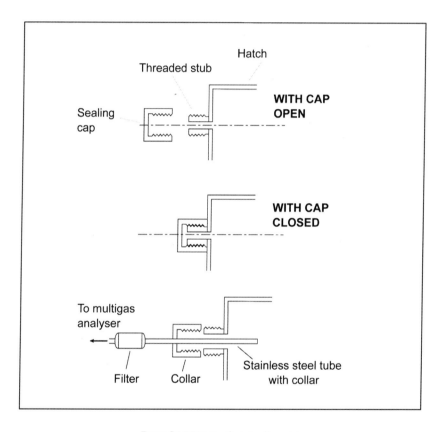

Figure G.2.7 *Diagram of gas sampling point*

Each sample point should comprise a hole of diameter approximately 12 mm positioned as near to the top of the hatch coaming as possible. It should be sealed with a screw cap to prevent ingress of water and air. It is essential that this cap is securely replaced after each measurement to maintain a tight seal.

The provision of any sample point should not compromise the seaworthiness of the vessel.

G.2.3 *Measurement*

Ensure that the instrument is calibrated and working properly in accordance with the manufacturer's instructions. Remove the sealing cap, insert the stainless steel tube into the sampling point and tighten the integral cap to ensure an adequate seal. Connect the instrument to the sampling tube. Draw a sample of the hold atmosphere through the tube, using the aspirator, until steady readings are obtained. Log the results on a form which records cargo hold, date and time for each measurement.

G.2.4 *Measurement strategy*

The identification of incipient self-heating from measurement of gas concentrations is more readily achieved under unventilated conditions. This is not always desirable because of the possibility of the accumulation of methane to dangerous concentrations. This is primarily, but not exclusively, a problem in the early stages of a voyage. Therefore it is recommended that holds are initially ventilated until measured methane concentrations are at an acceptably low level.

G.2.5 *Measurement in unventilated holds*

Under normal conditions one measurement per day is sufficient as a precautionary measure. However, if carbon monoxide levels are higher than 30 ppm then the frequency should be increased to at least twice a day at suitably spaced intervals. Any additional results should be logged.

If the carbon monoxide level in any hold reaches 50 ppm a self-heating condition may be developing and the owners of the vessel should be notified.

G.2.6 *Measurement in ventilated holds*

If the presence of methane is such that the ventilators are required to remain open, then a different procedure should be applied to enable the onset of any incipient self-heating to be detected.

▷ To obtain meaningful data the ventilators should be closed for a period before the measurements are taken. This period may be chosen to suit the operational requirements of the vessel, but it is recommended that it is not less than four hours. It is vital in the interests of data interpretation that the shutdown time is constant whichever time period is selected. These measurements should be taken on a daily basis. If the carbon monoxide results exhibit a steady rise over three consecutive days, or exceed 50 ppm on any day, the owners of the vessel should be notified. ◁

Maritime and Coastguard Agency

Carriage of coconut oil and other vegetable oils as cargo in tanks

Notice to Ship Owners, Operators and Managers, Masters and Officers of Merchant Ships and Offshore Installation Managers/Duty Holders and Shippers to the Offshore Industry

Summary

- Information has been received about unforeseen hazardous conditions that may arise when coconut oil and other vegetable oils are carried in the cargo or deep tanks of ships.

- This Marine Guidance Note draws attention to the hazards and makes recommendations to ensure safe working practices when handling such cargoes.

1. A report has been received about a serious accident that occurred on board a ship discharging a cargo of Indonesian crude coconut oil in a North European Port.

2. Six men hired from ashore entered one of the tanks nearing completion of discharge to sweep the residue towards the pump suction.

3. Within a few minutes, the workmen appeared to be in difficulties. Four were able to leave the tank but the other two collapsed over the heating coils. Both men suffered serious burns from the heating coils. One of them subsequently died.

4. The tank atmosphere was tested immediately after the accident for oxygen deficiency and flammability and found to be safe from those hazards.

5. However, very large concentrations of carbon monoxide (CO) were measured – more than 1000 – parts per million. As yet, there is no clear explanation for the presence of CO in the tank, though oxygen deficiency in tanks carrying such cargoes is well known.

6. A likely explanation is that the temperature of the heating coils had reached levels high enough to generate CO from the reducing quantity of cargo in the tank during the discharging process.

7. The Maritime and Coastguard Agency (MCA) therefore recommends that before such spaces are entered, the full range of precautions for entry into enclosed spaces described in the Code of Safe Working Practices for Merchant Seamen (section 17) or the International Maritime Organisation Assembly Resolution A.864(20) entitled Recommendations for Entering Enclosed Spaces Aboard Ship are observed.

8. The MCA also recommends that the atmosphere of cargo spaces with such oils are continuously monitored during the discharge process for the presence of CO if it is essential for personnel to be within that space. The temperature of the cargo should also be monitored closely. This is particularly important during the closing stages of the cargo discharge operation.

9. Carbon Monoxide is toxic by inhalation and can cause serious damage to health by prolonged exposure. Hence the 8 hour exposure limit for personnel to CO concentrations is 30 parts per million, though for short term exposure not exceeding 15 minutes, concentrations of up to 200 parts per million can be allowed.

10. Monitoring equipment should be capable of achieving the above degree of accuracy.

Environmental Quality Branch
Maritime and Coastguard Agency
Spring Place
105 Commercial Road
Southampton
SO15 1EG

Tel: 02380 329100
Fax: 02380 329204

File Ref: MS 116/032/0005

July 2002

Safer Lives, Safer Ships, Cleaner Seas

Department for
Transport

An executive agency of the
Department for Transport

mca

Maritime and Coastguard Agency

MGN 86 (M)

RECOMMENDATIONS ON THE SAFE USE OF PESTICIDES IN SHIPS

Notice to operators, shipowners, charterers, masters, agents, port and harbour authorities, shippers, container and vehicle packers, cargo terminal operators, fumigators, fumigant and pesticide manufacturers and all persons responsible for the unloading of freight containers

(This notice takes immediate effect)

Summary

The purpose of this guidance note is to advise on:

(1) the importance of safe and proper procedures when pesticides are used on board ships;

(2) the appropriate application of the IMO Recommendations on the Safe Use of Pesticides in Ships both to cargo and to cargo spaces; and

(3) to indicate the likely application of other related requirements or guidance which would be applicable to the use of, handling or transport of pesticides.

1. In accordance with the Merchant Shipping (Carriage of Cargoes) Regulations 1997[1], where pesticides are used in the cargo spaces of ships prior to, during, or following a voyage, the IMO publication "RECOMMENDATIONS ON THE SAFE USE OF PESTICIDES IN SHIPS" (1996 Edition, IMO267E), available from IMO, Publications Section, 4 Albert Embankment, London SE1 VSR where relevant thereto shall be complied with. The contents of this publication are also incorporated into the Supplement to the International Maritime Dangerous Goods (IMDG) Code. The use of pesticides includes the fumigation of cargo spaces and of cargo, in port, or in-transit, and any part of the ship so affected by their use, as contained in the Recommendations.

2. The Maritime and Coastguard Agency, in conjunction with the Ministry of Agriculture, [1]Fisheries and Food, the Scottish Office, Agriculture, Environment and Fisheries Department and the Health and Safety Executive, considers that it is essential that adequate precautions are taken by all those responsible for the commissioning of pest control on board ships. MCA strongly recommends observance of all the provisions contained in the Recommendations, but the necessity for the master and crew to cooperate with shore-based fumigation personnel in compliance with other safety requirements should be recognised. In the United Kingdom the Health and Safety Executive (HSE) is the relevant shore-based authority.

---

[1] S.I. 1997/No.19 as amended

3. Mandatory requirements cover the conditions for preparation and carriage of cargo transport units under fumigation. These are classified as Class 9 dangerous goods with the proper shipping name "CARGO TRANSPORT UNIT UNDER FUMIGATION" in the International Maritime Dangerous Goods (IMDG) Code, ("cargo transport unit" being any freight container or vehicle shipped under fumigation). The Merchant Shipping (Dangerous Goods and Marine Pollutants) Regulations 1997 require compliance with the IMDG Code for packaged dangerous goods for aspects such as declaration, stowage, segregation, marking, labelling and the display of a fumigation warning sign.

4. Pesticides, when not in use and carried as cargo may also be subject to the Regulations specified in paragraph 3 above and the IMDG Code.

5. The Recommendations regarding fumigation practice were written as a result of consultations with experts on pest control, pesticide safety and ship operation.

6. In one case, failure to comply with the recommended procedures caused a number of people to be hospitalised after exposure to phosphine gas generated in a cargo of grain fumigated with Aluminium Phosphide during the sea passage. The fumigant tablets were not fully decomposed and, hence, the fumigation process was not fully completed before the vessel arrived at the discharge port. There have also been a number of other incidents involving containerised cargoes arriving under fumigation at United Kingdom ports with no accompanying documentation on the ship or at the port of discharge regarding the nature of the cargo.

7. Merchant Shipping Notice MSN 1718 should be referred to for the statutory requirements on the safe use of pesticides (including fumigants), in cargo spaces on board ships when they are loaded or intended to be loaded with cargo. Although extensively referred to in these requirements, the scope and application of the IMO Recommendations is generally wider, providing, for example, guidance on the disinfestation of food stores, galleys and crew and passenger accommodation.

8. As pesticides are hazardous substances their handling and application and exposure to them are subject to regulations affecting the health and safety of workers at work. For further information other related documents should be referred to, e.g. Chapter 27 of the "Code of Safe Working Practices for Merchant Seamen"[2] and the Health and Safety Executive Approved Code of Practice (Control of Substances Hazardous to Health in Fumigation Operations"[3].

---

[2] Available from The Stationery Office
ISBN 0 11 5518363

[3] HSE Books ACOP L86 and also Guidance note on Fumigation CS22.

MSASD
Maritime and Coastguard Agency
Spring Place
Southampton SO15 1EG
August 1998

Tel: 01703 329 184
Fax: 01703 329 204

File reference: MS 116_31_028

DETR
ENVIRONMENT
TRANSPORT
REGIONS

An executive agency of the Department of the Environment, Transport and the Regions

mca
Maritime and Coastguard Agency

Inspection of Shell Loading Doors on Ro-Ro Ferries

Notice to: Ship Owners, Ship Builders, Certifying Authorities, Surveyors, Masters and Ships Officers.

Summary

This Guidance Note draws attention to the importance of crewmembers on-board Roll-on Roll-off ferries being aware of the position of the collision bulkhead and the need for it be kept fully intact whenever the ferry is at sea.

Key Points:

- Monthly inspections of shell loading doors
- Additional inspections immediately after every voyage where heavy weather has been encountered
- Notice boards drawing attention to the importance of the extended portion of the collision bulkhead and the need for it to be kept fully intact at sea
- The need for the extended portion of the collision bulkhead to be readily recognisable by crewmembers

1. Background

1.1 Following an incident, which occurred when a Roll-on Roll-off ferry encountered heavy weather whilst crossing the English Channel, damage was sustained to the shell loading door (bow visor). As a result, an investigation was carried out by the Marine Accident Investigation Branch (MAIB). The subsequent MAIB Report 1/8/18 was published and identified a number of recommendations.

1.2 This Guidance Note is intended to promulgate these recommendations to the relevant parties.

2. Collision Bulkheads

2.1 Due to their design and operations, certain vessels are required to have a collision bulkhead. This is a vertical bulkhead, of watertight construction, which extends from the keel to the bulkhead deck (ie usually the lower vehicle deck on a ro-ro ferry). It has to be located within strictly defined limits (e.g. not less than 5% of the length of the ship abaft the forward perpendicular). Its purpose is to give protection to the main body of the ship in the event of the fore end being breached due to collision or contact damage.

2.2 In addition, on ships which have a forward superstructure, for example the main vehicle space on a ro-ro passenger ferry, the collision bulkhead may be required to be extended weathertight to the next deck above. This extension need not be fitted directly over the bulkhead below, provided it is not less than 5% of the length of the ship from the forward perpendicular.

2.3 Where an extension of the collision bulkhead is required, it is of vital importance to the ro-ro passenger ferry. Primarily, it acts as a barrier to the ingress of sea water onto the vehicle decks should the fore end of the ship ever become breached due to collision or contact damage. In addition, it acts as a barrier to the ingress of sea water should the bow visor (or bow door) ever fail to function properly.

3 Crew Awareness

3.1 The MAIB investigation demonstrated the "vital importance which the extended portion of the collision bulkhead can play in the overall safety of ro-ro passenger ferries against the ingress of sea water." However the investigation also discovered that "only those crew with a very detailed knowledge of the ship's construction were likely to know of the exact location of the extended portion of the collision bulkhead. Moreover the Inspector was left with the impression that few of the ship's crew fully appreciated the importance the collision bulkhead plays in the overall safety of the ship. A situation which probably applies on most ro-ro ferries."

4. Recommendations

4.1 The recommendations made by the MAIB have been fully accepted by the Maritime & Coastguard Agency. These are produced in the following paragraphs.

4.2 All owners and managers of ro-ro passenger ferries should arrange for:-

- shell loading doors (e.g. bow visors and hinged bow and stern doors), which are required to be weathertight and fitted in their ferries, to be carefully inspected on a monthly basis and also after every voyage where heavy weather has been experienced.

- Any damage found to be quickly and effectively repaired.

- Records of such inspections to be retained for at least 12 months.

- The Maritime & Coastguard Agency to be promptly notified whenever an inspection reveals damage which could lead to the weathertight integrity being compromised.

4.3 All such ro-ro passenger ferries should have a notice board, placed in a suitable and prominent position on or near the bulkhead, which draws attention to the importance of the extension to the collision bulkhead and the need for it to be kept fully intact whenever the ferry is at sea.

4.4 The extended portion of the collision bulkhead on all ro-ro passenger ferries, especially when the layout is complicated, is to be readily recognisable to crew members, by special marking or painting, by use of diagrammatic sketches or by some other effective means.

5. Owners and managers should take due account of this guidance and ensure adequate record keeping and training of ship staff in accordance with the Safety Management System.

Survey Branch
105, Commercial Road
Southampton
SO15 1EG

Telephone: 023 80 329220
Fax: 023 80 329104
Internet: http://www.mcga.gov.uk

File Ref: MS008-008-1336

September 2002

Safer Lives, Safer Ships, Cleaner Seas

Department for Transport

mca
Maritime and Coastguard Agency

RECOMMENDATIONS FOR SHIPS CARRYING FUMIGATED BULK CARGOES

Notice to operators, shipowners, charterers, masters, agents, port and harbour authorities, shippers, bulk terminal operators, fumigators, fumigant manufacturers and all persons responsible for fumigating bulk cargos.

This MGN should be read in conjunction with MSN 1718, MGN 86 and the Merchant Shipping (Carriage of Cargoes) Regulations 1997 (as amended)

Summary

This guidance note advises on:

(1) the importance of safe and proper procedures when fumigants are used in bulk cargoes on board ships;
(2) the appropriate application of the IMO Recommendations on the Safe Use of Pesticides in ships carrying fumigated bulk cargoes; and
(3) the likely application of other related requirements or guidance that would be applicable to ships carrying fumigated bulk cargoes.

1.0 Introduction/ Background

1.1   This MGN has been produced to bring to the attention of ship's masters, owners, agents and port or terminal operators the dangers involved it the transportation and discharged of fumigated solid bulk cargoes.

2.0 Main points

IMO at DSC/Circl1 (available at the IMO website: http://www.imo.org) highlights the following points:

2.1   There may be an incorrect assumption that the concentration of the toxic fumigant in the holds and access ways of the ship is sufficiently low to avoid safety and health risks to ship and shore personnel or enforcement officers when the ship arrives in the port of discharge;

2.2   There are reported incidents where employees have been exposed to the fumigant, usually phosphine, causing health problems; and

2.3   Ships containing bulk cargo under fumigation, unlike in container transport units (CTUs), have no requirement to be labelled as such, and therefore may not be visibly recognised as a potential

1

health and safety risk. It should be noted that there is a requirement in the 'Code of Safe Practice for Merchant Seamen' to ensure that fumigation warning signs are conspicuously displayed on cargo units or spaces under fumigation.

3.0 The safe use of pesticides on ships

3.1. The International Convention for the Safety of Life at Sea (SOLAS) regulation VI/4, requires that appropriate precautions are taken in the use of pesticides in ships, in particular for the purposes of fumigation.

3.2 The Merchant Shipping (Carriage of Cargoes) Regulations 1997 require that where pesticides are used in the cargo spaces of ships prior to, or following a voyage, the IMO publication *Recommendations on the Safe Use of Pesticides in Ships* (2002 Edition) must be complied with. These regulations define 'the use of pesticides' to include the fumigation of cargo spaces and of cargo, in port, or in transit, and in any part of the ship or cargo so affected as a consequence of their application or use, as referred to in the 'Recommendations'.

3.3 To ensure compliance with the *Recommendations* detailed in 3.2 above all ships proceeding to a port within the United Kingdom, carrying solid bulk cargoes under fumigation, even if ventilation of the cargo has taken place during the voyage, must prior to arrival and in general not less than 24 hours in advance, inform either the port authority or terminal operator of the port or bulk terminal of destination that the bulk cargo has been fumigated. This information must be provided by either the ship's master, owner or the agent.

3.4 In cases where the presence of personnel in cargo spaces is required to ensure that fumigation tablets have fully decomposed before arrival at the discharge port, it is important that the Ship's master ensures that adequate respiratory protection (e.g. self contained compressed air breathing apparatus) is worn until all fumigation residues have been removed and the spaces have been thoroughly ventilated.

3.5 On arrival at any port within the United Kingdom where fumigated bulk cargo is to be discharged the master must establish the requirements of the port or bulk terminal regarding the handling of fumigated cargoes before any cargo is discharged. Before entry of fumigated cargo spaces, trained personnel from a fumigation company or other competent persons, wearing respiratory protection, must carry out careful monitoring of the spaces to ensure the safety of personnel. The monitoring values must be entered in the ships log book. The fumigation is not complete until the holds and cargo have been ventilated and tested and a certificate issued by a competent person stating that the cargo and holds are free from harmful concentrations of gas,

3.6 When the ship is found to be free of fumigants and certified as such, all warning signs should be removed. Any action in this respect should be recorded in the ship's log book

3.7 The precautions and procedures detailed in the 'Code of Safe Working Practises for Merchant Seamen' with regard to the entering of enclosed spaces should be taken in account.

3.8 The Merchant Shipping (International Safety Management (ISM) Code) Regulations 1998 require ships to develop plans for key shipboard operations concerning the safety of the ship and the prevention of pollution. These plans must include safety procedures for fumigation if the ship is likely to carry solid bulk cargo that may require fumigation.

4.0 Further Information

Further information on the contents of this MGN can be obtained from colin.thomas@mcga.gov.uk

(or the address at the end of this Notice)

Environmental Quality Branch
Maritime and Coastguard Agency
Spring Place
105 Commercial Road
SO15 1EG

Telephone: 023 8032 9402
Fax: 023 8032 9204
E-Mail: colin.thomas@mcga.gov.uk

General Enquiries: 24 Hour Info Line
infoline@mcga.gov.uk
0870 600 6505

MCA Website Address: Internet: http://www.mcga.gov.uk

File Ref: MS/41/16/14

Published: March 2005

© Crown Copyright 2005

Safer Lives, Safer Ships, Cleaner Seas

ISO 9001:2000
FS 34835

Department for
Transport

The MCA is an executive agency
of the Department for Transport

INDEX

BIBLIOGRAPHY

International Safety Guide for Oil Tankers and Terminals (ISGOTT)

Liquefied Gas Handling Principles on Ships and in Terminals - SIGTTO

Petroleum Tankship Cargo Handling Manual – Lorne & Maclean

Seamanship Techniques: Shipboard and Marine Operations, Third Edition – D. J. House. Published by Elsevier, 2004. ISBN: 0750663154

Cargo Work: For Maritime Operations – D. J. House. Published by Elsevier. ISBN: 0750665556

Refrigeration at Sea; Munton & Stott

Marine Refrigeration Manual; Capt Alders

Code of Safe Working Practices (COSWP) – MCA

www.containerhandbuch.de

Shipboard Petroleum Surveys; a guide to good practice

Glasgow College of Nautical Studies (GCNS) - Cargo work notes

ICS Tanker Safety Guide (Chemical)

The following HMSO Publications:

> SI 336 Carriage of Cargoes Regulation 1999
> SI 2151 Additional Safety Measures for Bulk Carriers
> Merchant Shipping (Hatches and Lifting Plant) Regulations 1988
> Merchant Shipping (Load Lines) Regulations 1988
> Merchant Shipping (Safe Loading and Unloading of Bulk Carriers) Regulations 2003
> Ro-Ro Vessels Stowage and Securing - HMSO

The following IMO publications:

> Inert Gas Systems, IMO
> BC Code
> BLU Code
> CSS Code
> IMDG Code
> IGC Code
> GC Code
> EGC Code
> IBC Code
> BCH Code
> International Grain Code
> Code of Safe Practice for Ships Carrying Timber Deck Cargoes

International Convention on Load Lines

Guidelines for the Preparation of Cargo Securing Manual

STCW' 95

SOLAS

MARPOL

Medical First Aid Guide (MFAG)

International Code for the Safe Carriage of Packaged Irradiated Nuclear Fuel (INF)

Specifications for the Design, Operation and Control of Crude Oil Washing Systems

Recommendations on the Safe Use of Pesticides at Sea

The Following Marine Guidance Notices (MGNs):

MGN 284

MGN 60

MGN 36